small apartment **hacks**

101 INGENIOUS DIY SOLUTIONS FOR LIVING, ORGANIZING, AND ENTERTAINING

JENNA MAHONEY

Published by
Ulysses Press
PO Box 3440
Berkeley, CA 94703
www.ulyssespress.com

ISBN: 978-1-64604-303-3
Library of Congress Catalog Number: 2013938634

Printed in the United States
10 9 8 7 6 5 4 3 2 1

Acquisitions editor: Katherine Furman
Editor: Mary Hern
Proofreader: Elyce Berrigan-Dunlop
Cover illustration: Timothy Collins
Front cover design: Rebecca Lown
Interior design and layout: Lindsay Tamura
Index: Sayre Van Young

contents

PART THREE: ENTERTAINING

introduction

There are nearly 25 million of us that live in apartments in the United States. And if builders' reports are true, and the average home sizes are getting smaller for the first time in decades—including those multi-dwelling spots we're crammed into—we've got even less living space in our future. Add in the newly developed big-city micro-apartment concept, and our living experience is looking a lot like *Alice's Adventures in Wonderland* (without the hedgehog croquet—we hope). But just like age ain't nothin' but a number, small square footage doesn't need to relegate your space to an overstuffed sausage. It's all about taking control of your belongings and finding what layouts work best for your space. With just a few habit changes, organization fixes, and design elements you can easily live large in a shoebox. After all, a man's home is his castle.

Defining your space. Defining yourself.

Before you start decorating, organizing, and hosting, you've got to make room to know yourself. Define your needs and wishes for your home. Realistically understand your capabilities. Sure, we'd all love to be as crafty as Martha Stewart and Erica Domesek of *PS I Made This* ..., but if you don't have the time, space or *actual* interest, you're only creating more mess—physically and mentally. And while we're on the subject, take some time to clear your mind while you're getting all this thinking going. A meditative spirit can help you feel centered and balanced, and in turn create a happy home.

Three-minute meditation

Sit quietly. That means you've got to turn off all the technology that's buzzing around you. Sit with a straight back, your head balanced evenly over your shoulders. Feet can be on the floor or folded under crossed legs. With eyes closed, focus your breath. Follow the sensation of the air as it enters you and passes throughout your lungs and body. Place one hand on your abdomen and follow the breath. Notice the sensations.

> *"Those who cannot change their minds cannot change anything."*
> —GEORGE BERNARD SHAW

Who are you?

Now that you're good and relaxed, it's time to think about what you really want out of your home. Step one in managing your space is a simple test of personality. Are you a yogi, a baker, a candlestick maker? Are you a DIY doyenne or a personal-style tumblr queen? Identify the three things that you love most—beauty products, baking cupcakes, reading first editions—and use them as the anchors to your design aesthetic and organization. For example: Surfers,

APARTMENT HISTORY FUN FACTS

Romans lived in apartments. Egyptians did, too.

Roman *plebs* (people of the lower to middle class of ancient Rome) lived in multi-family dwellings called *insula*. The first floor served as commercial space, while the top levels were living quarters. The lower units of the six- or seven-story buildings were more desirable.

Egyptian multiple-family, hi-rise dwellings date back to the fifth century. The buildings grew to as high as 14 stories in the 11th century and had rooftop gardens that were irrigated via ox-drawn water wheels.

It's believed that the rambling, yet precise, stone structures built by the ancient Chacoans of what is now New Mexico housed areas of worship, commercial spaces, and dwellings. The sophisticated buildings (circa 850–1250) contained up to 700 rooms spread over four to five stories.

Parisians of all classes have lived in apartments since the 17th century. Wealthier residents occupied the lower floors. Domestic workers lived in the upper attic quarters, which were accessible only by staircase.

Tenements on New York City's lower east side date back to the 1830s. The dwellings were mostly railroad style and housed immigrant workers. The first apartment building for the middle class was constructed in 1870s by Rutherford Stuyvesant, who sought to create the "French flat," an afford-able, communal living experience. The building boasted cold running water—a luxury at the time.

use your boards as design accents. Lean them up against the wall and hang your favorite caps and everyday totes from the nose. Fashionistas, use a wall as a gallery space for bags. Tack nails into a brick wall or affix hooks above your sofa and hang your most precious Chanel and Alexander Wang purses like the works of art they are.

Answer the questions

There's a Three Q Rule throughout this guide. Keep a cheat sheet in the notes section of your iPhone or on your desktop. When it comes to the items you already possess, as well as those that you're thinking of bringing into your tiny space, ask yourself these three questions.

1. What's its function?
2. How does it make me feel?
3. Would I save it in a fire?

Limit the amount of sentimental items in your possession—do you *really* need to hold on to that plastic cup from your first rock concert? Most things in your home should serve more than one purpose—you want to be able to call upon them to do double duty. Once you know you can honestly answer these questions for everything from bronzed baby booties to notes from high-school algebra, you're ready to start transforming your petite pad into a grand abode.

PART ONE:
ORGANIZING

"Simplicity is the ultimate sophistication."
—LEONARDO DA VINCI

getting your hands dirty

Before you can get into the fun part of implementing inge-
nius new apartment solutions, there's some elbow grease
that needs to be worked into your space.

Have a vision

Like most things in life, pulling your small space together
needs a plan. Avoid a hodgepodge of style, stuff, and furniture that just looks like an overcrowded mishmash. Write
down three goals for your living quarters: Do you want it
to look chic, streamlined, and modern? Cozy, vintage, and
sunny? Use your answers to "Who are you?" on page 2
as a guide. Having the broad stroke concepts will aid in
furniture selection. Beware of falling into the match trap.
Being too matchy-matchy can make a small space look like
a mini-version of a furniture showroom. Instead, pick pieces
that blend in color and balance in scale and proportion.
Later, introduce items of unifying color and style.

> *"In order to seek one's own direction,*
> *one must simplify the mechanics of*
> *ordinary, everyday life."*
> —PLATO

Declutter

Fact: Piles of paper, mountains of magazines, and inessential stuff accounts for 40% of the cleaning needs in American households. Getting rid of clutter not only tidies up your space, it also decreases stress. Psychologists say having a disordered home can lead to feelings of anxiety, guilt, and other not-so-fun stuff like the inability to properly relax. Take a deep breath. Getting rid of the mess is the easy part; it's keeping it that way that can be the challenge.

SPEED CLEAN IN THREE STEPS

1. **Contain the clutter.** Use a basket to collect stuff that's floating where it shouldn't be. Return the items to their proper place in your home and pitch those that you don't need. Old receipts, we're talking to you.

2. **Dust and vacuum.** Everything looks drearier (and dirtier) with even a light sprinkling of dust. Quickly run a microfiber cloth over tables, bookcases, and shelves. (The fabric traps bitty bunnies.) Further spiff up with a speedy vacuum sweep over the floors and fabric furniture.

3. **Wipe down.** The bathroom and kitchen can easily get a one-way ticket to grime city. Luckily, stopping them before take-off is easy. After preparing food, run a sponge over the stove, countertop, and sink. Use an antibacterial, pre-moistened towelette to wipe down the bathroom sink, tub, and toilet once a day.

Tip: Declutter one space, one room, one drawer at a time. Attempting to multitask will just create a jumble of both your things and your mindset.

> *"Simplify. Simplify."*
> —DAVID HENRY THOREAU

Just do it

Procrastination doesn't benefit anyone. Make it a habit to deal with tasks immediately. There are no dishwashing fairies, nor will the *Cinderella* birds help sweep away the dust. And let's be real, the longer you wait, the worse it gets— caked-on, weird foodstuff requires way more elbow grease. So instead of setting yourself up for hard labor down the line, sort and toss mail as it arrives and return anything that you use to its proper home upon completion. Remember: It's just as easy to toss your day's outfit on the floor as it is to place it back in the closet. If you can't let go of the I'll-just-leave-it-for-now mentality, see "Make a landing strip" on page 14.

> *"True life is lived when tiny changes occur."*
> —LEO TOLSTOY

Make dates

When it comes to exercise, healthy eating, and other good habits, a slew of studies show you're more likely to stick with something if you schedule it—in pen. (Since a paper planner can add to the clutter, make cleaning appointments in your Google calendar with reminders.) Schedule a deep house clean—floors, bathroom, and inside of the fridge—twice a month. Set aside a couple of hours (Saturday mornings before yoga are a great time). Put on your favorite music, podcast, or book-on-tape to stoke your energy throughout the project. See "Clean Green" on page 56 for tips on scrubbing up in a healthy way.

Similarly, make reorg appointments with yourself quarterly. Review the "Toss, Store, Keep" strategies found on page 15. If something isn't working—like your kitchen accessories drawer is out of reach, or your landing strips (page 14) have been abandoned for landing fields across various surfaces—come up with a new method. A key to remaining clutter-free is having an easy system that actually works for your lifestyle and home.

> *"To improve is to change;*
> *to be perfect is to change often."*
> — WINSTON CHURCHILL

your better
(or worse) half

No matter how good (or bad) your relationship is with the person you live with, it's rare that you'll perfectly see eye-to-eye on design and cleaning habits. Having a straightforward plan in place for décor and chore delegation is easier than trying to tackle things issue by issue, which will just end up making you seem like a nag.

How to combine your stuff

You've had the move-in talk, so now it's time to chat about the merge. According to a survey conducted by eBay Classifieds, 54% of Americans have ten duplicate items when they move in with a significant other. So whether it's with a random roomie, a long-time partner, or an age-old bestie, odds are it's time to trim the fat.

Take stock. Make an inventory list of furniture and appliances. Use your personality quiz on page 2 and your space vision on page 6 to figure out what you need, and what can realistically fit in the space.

Vote. Start with the doubles. Whose coffeemaker is in better shape? Who is more attached to their grandmother's silver? Then whittle down the single items like vases and clocks that may take up space in the combined home.

Start over. If you can't agree on whose couch is cuter, it may be time to choose a new one. Together, decide on items that physically fit your home as well as suit both of your personalities.

Share the space. Remember this is now a joint home, which means you should both feel comfortable in the abode. Items should reflect both of you and your combined needs.

SQUARE FOOTAGE STATISTICS

What's an apartment? It depends on where you go. Here are some of the minimum living sizes in cities across the world:

- *Boston:* 450 square feet
- *Buenos Aires:* 96.8 square feet
- *Chicago:* 125 square feet
- *Los Angeles:* 250 square feet
- *Miami:* 950 square feet
- *New York City:* 400 square feet
- *Paris:* 96.8 square feet
- *San Francisco:* 290 square feet

But the future is small; here are proposed sizes for micro apartments in some U.S. cities:

- *Boston:* 300 square feet versus current legal size of 450 square feet
- *New York City:* 250 square feet versus current legal size of 400 square feet
- *San Francisco:* 220 square feet versus current legal size of 290 square feet

Three tricks for dealing with a messy roomie (or spouse!)

There's a lot of things you love about them, but the frequency with which they clean the bathroom may not be one of them.

1. **Divide my-side, your-side.** Define your space and your roomie's. Be direct about your cleanliness expectations and discuss doable—and realistic—chore division. If you're the one starting the negotiations, try not to be overbearing when you talk, or you may just make the issue messier.

2. **Distinguish between filth and mess.** One is potentially dangerous (toxic mold, vermin, oh my!), the other is simply annoying. If the problem is a messy Jesse, create a catchall box for his stuff. When you do a speed clean, put all of his items in a basket and place it on his side of the room.

3. **Hire a pro.** Forget fighting over the chore wheel and pool your resources for a bimonthly deep clean. Bonus: It'll alleviate your urge to nag.

Note: Safety hazards should be addressed with your landlord or dorm manager.

"Housekeeping ain't no joke."
—LOUISA MAY ALCOTT

good practices

You know who you are—you've found a bit of mindful calm and gained a vision of your space (and the one you're living with if that's where you're at), but before you can put on your decorator's cap, you've got to get organized. If you're easily distracted, set an alarm on your phone to help focus your time limits.

Create zones

Whether you live in a 375-square-foot studio or a 1,200-square-foot two-bedroom apartment, the number one key to keeping it clean, pretty, and functioning is assigning a home base for everything you own. Cordon off areas that serve specific purposes and place anything that corresponds to such there. Obviously, the kitchen is for cooking and eating, but are you a crafter that uses the stove and sink a lot? Think about allocating a drawer or overhead cabinet space exclusively for your tools for projects. If you don't have space for a desk, delineate a portion of your credenza or bedside table as your tech center (page 36). Immediately remove anything that doesn't correspond to the zone. And strictly stick to a zone's function and use.

Make a landing strip

Let's face it—no one's home *actually* looks like a real estate listing at all times. And there are very few people who can realistically keep their places looking visitor-perfect 24/7. Avoid creating chaos by containing your procrastination to a landing strip. Use the top of your desk or a surface by your entrance to stack mail and other papers that you don't feel like dealing with immediately. Once a week, edit the pile, recycle or shred the garbage, and respond to any formal invitations and bills. You may also consider a landing strip in your bedroom area. Choose a chair or bench to drop yesterday's outfit, this morning's gym clothes, and last night's date night pumps in a single place. Clean it off weekly, or the aforementioned chaos will ensue.

toss, store, keep

MAJOR PROJECT ALERT! It's time to use the Three Q Rule in every room of your home. Here is a room-by-room guide that will help you. Take out every item you own, hold it up, and ask yourself three questions: Does this have a function? When's the last time I used it? How does it make me feel? If you can't define any of the three, that's an immediate toss. If it has an actual function but you don't particularly love it (like that beat-up TV stand your boyfriend brought from his frat house), hold onto it until you've found a suitable replacement. While there are places in every home for sentimental items that don't really have a purpose, your house is not the museum of you. It's a living space and if your stuff gets in the way, you're defeating yourself. It's a good idea to have four boxes or piles when examining each subject. Label them: Keep, Trash, Donate, and Put Away (for items that don't live in the drawer you found it in). Aim to do this practice once quarterly.

clothing

If Michelle Obama and Anna Wintour can repeat their favorite cardigans and sling backs, so can you. An over-stuffed closet doesn't actually give more outfit options, just more—you guessed it—clutter. Immediately toss anything that's stained beyond salvation. Edit your closet using Three Clothing Qs:

1. **Have I worn this in the past year?** If yes, and it fits, it stays. If the answer is no, you need to do further investigation. If you haven't put it on in 18 months, no further thought is needed; it should get recycled. See "Where to Toss" on page 41.

2. **Is this piece classic?** Blue blazers, black cardigans, and crisp white shirts are always in season for men and women. The same can be said for ballet flats and tailored jeans (see "Six clothing items every woman should own" on page 17 and "Seven clothing items every guy should own" on page 18 for classic closet pieces). Get rid of any items that scream, "Hey! I'm from the Nixon administration" or "I went on tour with the Grateful Dead" or "Does anyone know the way to West Beverly High, you know, 90210?" Vintage items that have a classic shape and structure can stay. If Audrey Hepburn or George Clooney would wear

the piece in question, it's a keeper. One exception to the classic keeper rule: if you answer "no" to the next question.

3. **Does it fit?** Don't keep things that you think you may wear one day when you lose those last seven pounds. And don't hang onto anything that makes you look anything less than your best. Text friends images of yourself in pieces that you're on the fence about.

If the item has sentimental value (more it-belonged-to-a-relative and less I-met-the-person-I'm-currently-dating-wearing-this-flannel) and finally—this is key!—if it is well made, it can stay. Classic, special occasion items (a vintage fur wrap, a cashmere car coat) can live in your closet for years without use.

"Trends may come and go, but style is forever."
—YVES SAINT LAURENT

Six clothing items every woman should own

1. **LBD.** Office, event, even courtroom appropriate, the little black dress is a number-one must-have on every fashion editor's need list. Choose a sheath; it can be worn day or night.

2. **Black or navy blazer.** A well-cut jacket pairs with everything from jeans to LBDs. Choose a style that

accentuates the waist. Shy away from styles with span-gled buttons, which can look dated.

3. **Dark wash jeans.** Faded washes can look juvenile and inappropriate, while deep rinse denim can go from the office and happy hour to the playground. A fitted, flared cut jean is universally flattering and elongates the leg.

4. **Trench coat.** Another classic and timeless outfit transformer, a belted trench can finish any look. Bonus: The well-fashioned coat can fit across fluxes in weight.

5. **Tailored, collared shirt.** The consistent theme with the items on this list is that they all make you look chic and effortlessly polished. A crisp white shirt with French cuffs adds a bit of sophistication to any bottom choice, including jeans.

6. **Neutral cashmere sweater.** Simultaneously warm and lightweight, a gray or caramel V-neck can layer without bulk.

Seven clothing items every guy should own

Getting that classic, handsome-guy look is easier than you think.

1. **Navy suit.** A lightweight, wool navy suit is not only classic, it can be worn in any season, for any occasion (wedding, job interview, court appear-ance). Keep the look timeless with a single-breast,

three-button jacket. Another tip: Opt for flat-front, cuff-less pants.

2. **Black dress shoes.** You can't exactly pair your spiffy suit with a pair of trainers, right? The black shoe in an oxford style is appropriate footwear for both the office and evening. Choose shoes with minimal stitching to retain a sense of timelessness.

3. **Blue dress shirt.** A white shirt can look too formal with your suit, while a well-tailored, light blue oxford pairs with a suit, chinos, and jeans. It can even work under a hoodie. Brooks Brothers makes a non-iron version, which can be tossed in a suitcase or gym bag without the worry of wrinkles.

4. **Chinos/khaki pants.** It's been said that these pants are so versatile you can sleep in them. Technically speaking, khakis are the more causal of the two, but err on the side of Dockers for a universally flattering fit in natural cotton twill. Chinos look best with flat fronts. Hem or roll any styles that are too long in the leg. Bonus: You don't need to iron them.

5. **Neutral V-neck sweater.** Wear to the bars or to the office. Fact: Collared shirts fit better under V-necks than crew styles. Choose a cut that fits the collar well while still working with a causal T. Lightweight cashmere is perfect for a more formal look. Navy pairs well with khakis as well as jeans.

6. **Canvas sneakers.** Running shoes are too "I'm lifting later" and the toe shoes don't translate into any situa-

tion well. A neutral canvas sneak is cool for attending game night or a night game. Depending on your profession, they may also work on casual days.

7. **Leather jacket.** Everybody's got a bit of badass in him. A well-cut leather jacket looks good in any situation that doesn't require a suit. Look for slim cut styles with limited hardware.

(SOME) SYNONYMS FOR SMALL

When you find yourself trying to describe your apartment, you can get a lot more creative than just saying it's small. You could tell people it's …

baby	Lilliputian	narrow	slight
bantam	limited	petite	small-scale
bite-sized	little	picayune	spare
bitty	micro	piddling	sparse
cozy	microscopic	pint-sized	teensy
dinky	mini	pocket-sized	teeny
dwarfish	miniature	puny	toy
fine	minikin	runty	toylike
half-pint	minim	scanty	trifling
intimate	minute	scrubby	trivial
itsy-bitsy	modest	shrimpy	wee

You may also see some of these words pop up in descriptions from the real estate section as synonyms for "not a whole lotta square feet."

The difference between dated and vintage

Vintage is the catchall term for second-hand clothing or first-run garments from a prior era. Vintage clothing tends to be classic in shape and style and holds up when removed from its original time period. Generally speaking, clothing that dates from before the 1920s is called antique.

Keeping (and shopping for) vintage pieces can be a bit tricky, since the wrong move can make clothes appear out of step. Three tips to dealing with old clothes:

1. **Be a label snob.** Designer pieces and natural fibers keep their shape over the years. Look for the union card on the inseam. Usually square and about ½ inch by ½ inch, these indicate the garment was constructed in the U.S. before the 1980s. Common tags read "Ladies Garment Workers Union" and "Made in U.S.A."

2. **Keep it "modern."** Choose solid colors over patterned pieces. Large graphics can look dated.

3. **Inspect the hardware.** Tears, catches, and missing zipper teeth can look sloppy. Skip buying bags, shoes, or scarves unless they are perfect. Ditto for fit on sweaters, pants, and skirts.

> *"Fashion changes, but style endures."*
> —COCO CHANEL

furniture

Like your clothing, furniture is meant to be functional as well as stylish. If it's too much of one and not enough of the other, you've got a problem. When furnishings don't fit physically or if they jam up the sense of flow in your home, your space feels even more like a matchbox. Since furniture is both big in size and investment, it can be a little more difficult to part with pieces that aren't working, but you can do it. Toss anything that's stained or severely damaged. Scratches on wooden tables can be sanded down, but gashes in upholstery may call for a pro. (See "Clever reuse" on page 49 for tips on how to give your things a new life.) Use the Three Furniture Qs to make the break. It's easier than you think—promise!

1. **What's the function?** Duh, the sofa's job is to be a place to sit, chat, watch TV, use my laptop, and sometimes sleep. But the point here is: Does the couch easily transform into a bed? Does it have built-in storage? Aim to have pieces that are not only multitaskers, but that can also be used in a variety of situations. Ottomans with storage compartments can be used as an extra seat, coffee table, footrest, or bedside table.

2. **Does it fit?** Nothing screams, "Welcome to tiny town!" like oversize, prominent TV or computer screens. If

you aren't Kevin Spacey or Shonda Rhimes, do you really need the largest flat-panel LCD in town? How about that sectional you just tripped over on the way to your desk? Massive pieces not only hog precious real estate, they also make small areas appear more miniscule.

3. **How does it make me feel?** If your desk-slash-dinner table-slash-crafting area makes your face do The Scream every time it catches your eye, it may be time to say bye-bye. Yes, the table is super functional, and sure it fits in the space, but the key to building a home is making it feel, well, homey. Carefully select items that not only serve a function (preferably double duty), but also make you feel happy.

Three apartment necessities

Every apartment needs to address these necessities to be called home. All the other stuff is gravy.

1. **Sleep.** Home may be where the heart is, but it is also fundamentally the place where we rest our weary heads. And having a dedicated sleeping space is key to creating a home. Whether it's a Murphy bed or a California King, your crib needs a bed that's comfortable and functional. (P.S. We spend a third of our life sleeping, so we might as well do it sweetly.)

2. **Sit.** Your bed doesn't count. Everyone needs a place to have a moment of repose. A sofa, wingback, Eames, or recliner is the perfect perch to watch TV, read a book, put on your shoes, or simply daydream.

STEPS TO MEASURE A ROOM

1. To get the most precise measurement, use a 50-foot tape measure with the assistance of a friend. That way you'll have help keeping it straight—a biggie to assure precision—and you'll have enough tape to measure long walls if necessary.
2. Measure the width and height of walls, and the length of the floors. To ensure you've got an actual square, and not a curvature, measure diagonally from corner to corner.
3. Run the tape over the windows, length-wise and width-wise. Note how far the windows are from the floor and tops of the ceiling. Also measure around radiators, if they take up floor space.

3. **Eat.** Having a sturdy, dedicated place to enjoy the fruits of your labor and the bacon it brings home isn't merely adult, it's human. But not everyone needs a banquet table. Choose a table that fits your space and lifestyle.

> *"Home is the nicest word there is."*
> —LAURA INGALLS WILDER

The low-down on furniture wood

Generally speaking, furniture is constructed of three types of wood—hard, soft, and engineered.

Hardwood. Sourced from deciduous trees—oak, maple, mahogany, teak, walnut, cherry, and birch—pieces of this type are sturdy. The wood tends to be air- and kiln-dried to remove all moisture. Furniture made of hardwood is the most expensive (and heaviest to move, which is good to keep in mind if you're still sort of transient).

Softwood. Coniferous trees such as fir, cedar, and pine tend to have a reddish or yellow color. Since they grow quickly, furniture of this type is less expensive than hardwood. Softwoods tend to scratch or dent easily, therefore they need more care.

Veneer. Thin layers of various woods are adhered to plywood or other materials to create a wood-finish appearance. The benefit of this process is to curb consumer cost. Some furniture comes in multiple woods, which is a combo of high and low. Often, cheaper legs will be stained to match a higher quality tabletop.

kitchen

The hearth is the heart of the home. The kitchen feeds us both literally and figuratively. Not only should it be spick-and-span clean at all times, but your kitchen area should also reflect a healthy life view. And as we know, a decluttered space is a balanced space; use the Three Kitchen Qs to achieve that.

1. **How long has it been here?** Most foods, even canned ones, have a shelf life. Captain Obvious, right? But you'd be surprised how many out-of-date cans and bottles are taking up valuable cabinet real estate. Although you can hold on to many of them for up to 18 months, aim to consume canned food within a year of purchase. Some low-acid foods can be stored for two to five years. Immediately toss tins that are broken, punctured, bulged, or rusted, as they may have botulism. Make sure you properly dispose of expired jarred foods, so that no human or animal will consume them. Place the can in a double plastic bag and tape it closed. Handle with gloves if opened or punctured.

   Flour, sugar, and other dry goods should be bug-free. Throw out anything that smells rancid. Since baking powder and many spices can lose their potency,

FOOD LIFERS

If stored properly, some foods can stay (nearly) forever in the cabinet. Seal the following in airtight containers in a cool area away from sunlight, and you'll be set for life.

Honey. Sweet news: This treat is edible indefinitely. If it crystallizes, simply place the opened jar in a pot of water at medium heat. Stir honey until you like the viscosity. Extend the shelf life of honey's sweet cousin, maple syrup, by storing it in the freezer.

Pure vanilla extract. The expensive powerhouse counterpart to the imitation called for in nearly all baked goods is the Energizer bunny of the spice rack.

Rice. As long as it's contaminant-free, you can enjoy your favorite rice (no matter the grain) whenever you like. However, the oil content in brown rice makes its lifespan a little shorter.

Hard liquor. Although the taste and aroma fade gradually over time, distilled spirits can still be enjoyed in a snifter or in a favorite recipe.

Distilled white vinegar. The ultimate kitchen multitasker has incredible longevity.

Salt. There's a reason it's the world's oldest spice—it never goes stale.

restock every six months. And just like aspirational clothes, aspirational foods—goji berries, cold-pressed flax oil, a lifetime supply of chia—need to be given the heave-ho if you don't actually eat them.

2. **Is it chipped?** If you can repurpose the bone china teacup or the Liberty print salad plate, you can consider keeping it. But generally speaking, anything that's broken gets the *hasta luego* treatment. Teacups make cute votive holders, bud vases, or bathroom vanity storage for bobby pins and hair elastics. Place those old plates under plants to catch water. However, don't fall into the sentimental trap. If you can't think of a different use immediately, sorry, Charlie, it doesn't make the cut. Ditto for mismatched items, rusted or bent silverware, and warped cutting boards.

3. **What's its function?** The Vitamix makes juices, the KitchenAid mixer makes pasta, and the toaster makes toast, but do you use any of those items more than once a week? If the answer is yes, the item stays. Do you make it less than once a quarter? Umm … well, then it's time for a Craigslist post. In addition to tossing the specialty items that aren't used, it's time to chuck the cookbooks that should be renamed dustbooks. Scan or clip any recipes you do use and collate them into a single book or onto your tablet. Edit your mountain of plastic containers. Toss any that don't have tops or are warped. Trash excess covers, too. Donate or yard sale the pineapple corer, the knives that barely cut butter, and anything else that doesn't adequately perform its function (see "Where to Toss" on page 41).

*According to the Duke Center on Sustainability,
14% of home food purchases are wasted due to
either spoilage or being discarded as scraps.*

How to clean cookware

Enamel. Although the label may say "dishwasher safe," it's best to hand wash with a sponge and warm soapy water. A soak may be necessary to remove stuck-on residue. Make sure the pan is properly cooled before placing under cold water, or you run the risk of cracking the enamel.

Copper. Sponge down directly after use with warm water and soap. To avoid discoloring, use a copper cleaner to polish the pan.

Stainless steel. Clean immediately with a sponge and soap and water. Remove stuck-on food or stubborn stains with a powdered cleaner. Rinse with warm water until there is no longer the sensation of grit.

Nonstick. Never use scouring pads or powdered cleaners, which can damage the coating. Instead clean with soapy water and a soft sponge.

bathroom and linens

Yes, it's ground zero for personal business and grooming, but the washroom is also a place for relaxation. Come on, admit it, you've often dreamed of having a spa or a steam room at home. Now, I can't give you an extra-deep, jetted tub-for-two in your teensy space, but getting rid of the excess stuff and clearing off the surfaces will instantly infuse your bathroom with a sense of calm. Starting with the medicine chest and moving down through the vanity and its surfaces, use the Three Bathroom Qs.

1. **How often do you use it?** Let's be real. If the last time you used that crimp iron was when a Pat Benetar video debuted, get rid of it. Ditto for the hand cream you bought on that ski vacation three seasons ago. Small spaces seem even itsy bitsier when shelves are packed. Toss any partially-used products that aren't in the current rotation. (See "When to bin personal products" on page 33.) Send most of your sample sizes straight to see-you-later town. The exception—if you host out-of-town guests, use a few to create a bathroom caddy (see page 127). Check the expiration date on medicines and make sure your OTCs are current.

2. **How many do you really need?** So you've got a lip balm addiction, but do you actually require eight tins

of Rosebud Salve, sixteen Chapsticks, and some other rando brands you picked up because you liked the packaging? Take out the doubles, trips, and quads of items. Toss anything beyond its prime. (You should have done that in step one, but I know you felt like you needed that extra bottle of shampoo, just in case.) So, pitch it now. Then allow yourself to keep a single back up. (The exception here is toilet paper.) Place the rest of the unused items in a box for donation. See "Where to Toss" on page 41 for where to donate. Also remove anything from the bathroom that doesn't really belong there, such as excess decorative pieces. Again, a sleek space is a serene one.

3. **What is the condition?** Bath linens that are stained or torn look dumpy. And that's no way to feel after cleansing. Toss anything that's threadbare while you are at it. Again, get rid of excess. Chances are you aren't going to be hosting a platoon in your tiny apartment, so do you really need a dozen bath towels?

Three ways to safely dispose of drugs

1. **Turn them in.** Your best bet for pitching old meds responsibly is a medicine take-back program. Call your local landfill or go to the U.S. Drug Enforcement Administration's website (justice.gov) for details.

2. **Mix it up.** Take the old drugs and combine them with kitty litter or used coffee grounds so they're too messed up for anyone (or any pet) to get into. Place the mixture in a sealed Ziploc bag and toss it in your

garbage can. Do not crush the pills. Note: Medicated patches cannot be disposed of in this manner.

3. **Flush 'em.** Because they can be lethal to those who don't have a prescription but use them anyway, some medications need to be disposed of immediately. Older ones, however, are a bit trickier, as some medications can cause more harm in the water stream. Go to fda.gov for a list of flushable meds.

EVERY HOUSE SHOULD HAVE A FIRST AID KIT

Get a waterproof, spill-proof container. In it, divide supplies into two bags—wound supplies and medications—along with important medical contact and insurance info.

Wound Supplies
- Ace bandage
- Adhesive tape
- Band-Aids, all sizes
- Non-adhesive pads (for covering burns)
- Safety pins
- Scissors
- Sterile gauze pads
- Tweezers

Medications
- Anesthetic spray or lotion (for bug bites or itchy rashes)
- Antibiotic topical cream (for cuts and simple wounds)
- Antiseptic wipes
- Hydrocortisone ointment
- Oral antihistamine

Note: No matter how you dispose of your drugs, make sure you black out the prescription info.

When to bin personal products

Holding onto the shaving kit you got when you first sprouted stubble or that glitter eye shadow you bought for the *NSYNC concert is not only a clutter problem, it's an icky issue. Old personal care products are bacteria breeding grounds. Skin care products can also lose efficacy over time.

When to toss

PRODUCT	TIME AFTER PURCHASE
Acne products	6 months (or on expiration date)
Aftershave	When scent is gone (or on expiration date)
Broad-spectrum sunscreen	6 months (or on expiration date)
Cream blush or shadow	8 months
Deodorant	1 to 2 years after opening (or on expiration date)
Disposable razor	1 week (after use)
Eye pencil	1 year
Fragrance	1 to 2 years
Lipstick and gloss	2 years
Liquid foundation	6 months
Loofah	3 months
Loose powder	2 years
Mascara	3 months
Nail polish	2 years
Shampoo & conditioner	1 year
Toothpaste	1 year (or expiration date)

office and paperwork

It's alive! OK, that's a bit of an exaggeration, but oftentimes the leaning tower of mail, important docs, and photos on your desk (or portion of your kitchen counter that catches your paperwork) can become overwhelming. Excess paper is the number-one source of clutter in our homes. And like a bad weed, it spreads. Seriously, check and see if you've got paper in the bathroom, bedroom, kitchen, living area, and, oh, is that a newspaper in your bed? Use the Three Office Qs to edit your mail landing strip (see page 14) and VIP (very important paper) piles. Paying any bills and responding to invitations immediately is important, so put the info in your iCal. Depending on your clutterbug tendencies, you may need to do a monthly paper purge as opposed to a quarterly one for the other areas of your home.

1. **Will I need it again?** There are few documents that are actually necessary to keep on file. Tax documents are one. Also hold onto mortgage, credit card, bank, and investment statements for a lucky seven years. Same goes for deductible business receipts and bills. Store warranties and user guides together in an accessible spot. Label everything and, if you've got space, collect the documents into binders. Now let's talk about all those receipts from the nail salon, the

drugstore, heath food store, puppy food supply place, magazine kiosk, and last week's happy hour. If they aren't business expenses or deductible,what are they doing? The quick answer: gathering dust. Shred any documents and junk mail that have sensitive materials. Reuse the shredded paper to store fragile items like Christmas ornaments. Have old newspapers around? Use the pages to store sweaters (it can keep moths away).

Give catalogs, magazines, and unused clippings the recycle treatment, or better yet use them as wrapping paper. If you're holding onto the Crate and Barrel and Antropologie catalogs for décor inspiration, rip out the pertinent pages. Label and create a folder for the tear sheets. Do the same for fashion cut-outs, recipes, craft projects, and the like from magazines and newspapers. No need to go overboard-Type-A with the labels; do what you find appropriate not what you think someone else would do. Color-code the folders for easier organization. If you store photos and private letters in your office area, use the Three Sentimental Qs on page 46 for handling those items.

2. **Can it be digitized?** When was the last time you popped in a DVD or mix tape? Move your favorite Veronica Mars episodes onto your hard drive and upload all your music as well. Scan mortgage statements, receipts, and bills that need to be stored for tax purposes. Even better, precycle papers by signing up

for paperless billing. Come tax time, you can simply print the statements from your inbox. Consider paying your bills online and opt for e-mailed receipts when possible. If you use American Express, they offer a handy end-of-the-year function that categorizes your transactions. Go through your piles of thumb drives. Consolidate what you can onto a few and recycle the rest. They are serious drawer junkers. While you're at it, sweep up your inboxes as well. Remember: A streamlined system promotes a calm mind.

3. **What does that cord attach to?** Admit it, that bundle of wires at the back of your desk has been there since the PalmPilot launched. Clear out any chargers and reusable batteries that correspond to technology that dates to the first Bush presidency. Unused cell phones, CD players, and iPods should be properly recycled. See "Where to Toss" on page 41 for tips. Get rid of broken cords, non-functioning plugs, and anything else that doesn't work.

Create a tech center

Invest in some cord tamers or make your own (see "DIY Cord Storage" on page 37). Harness all chargeable devices and juice them up at a designated docking station. Consider tagging plugs with ID stickers. Use an old paper towel roll to store extension cords that aren't in use. See that cassette tape case you're about to toss? It's the perfect see-through container for iPlugs and the iPod factory-issue

CLUTTER BY THE NUMBERS

- An approximate 44% of junk mail is never opened. Call 888-5OPTOUT to get off credit card solicitation lists. Email optout@abacus-direct.com to stop the stream of unwanted catalogs.
- Twenty-three percent of adults pay bills late because they can't find them. Go paperless for statements and bills or consider enrolling in automatic payment plans.
- According to the National Association of Professional Organizers, we spend one year of our lives looking for lost items.
- A twelve-foot-high wall could be built from New York City to Los Angeles with all of the paper thrown out in the U.S. each year.

headphones. If you need batteries for anything, store them nearby.

DIY cord storage

Cord Catchall. Yoke all your juicers into a single unit behind your desk (or credenza or wherever you've zoned your tech center.) Still have your Blockbuster card or some other laminated detritus that's in disuse? With a hole-puncher, punch as many holes as you have gadgets. Cut a single slice from the edge to each hole with scissors, and slide in your cards. Admittedly it isn't the sturdiest solution, but it's better than attack of the killer cords. If you're concerned about the aesthetics, spray the card with a quick hit of paint.

Cord Box. Tame the DVD, TV, computer output cable, and the like in a DIY box. A cardboard media box (found at the Container Store, Home Goods, or on Amazon) works best because it's sturdy, but in a pinch a shoebox can function as well. With an X-Acto knife, cut out as many holes as plugs. Reinforce each hole with a bookplate (found at any craft store) or other sturdy sticker. Place a power strip in the box and plug everything in. Label each hole. Note: Monitor the box to ensure it doesn't get too hot.

THREE RULES TO DIY

Nearly 7% of us have been living with unfinished DIY projects for more than two years. Don't be a statistic.

1. Finish what you started. Don't start a new project until you've completed any works in progress. Write down whatever is outstanding, and prioritize the list. If there's anything you realistically aren't going to finish, either hire someone to do it for you or toss it.

2. Manage your expectations. Before you take on a new DIY, ask yourself: Do I have the skills and tools to do this? What is a realistic timeline to complete the project? And do I have the space in my home to do this?

3. Enlist a partner. Sometimes it's easier to get motivated and stick to a schedule when you've got a teammate. If you'd rather work alone, set crafting dates in your calendar.

Docking Station. Thoroughly clean out a flat-shaped plastic bottle (shampoo or moisturizer bottles work well). Using your phone as a measuring tool, sketch out the shape and size you'd like the cradle to be. It is a good idea to keep the front lower, so you can see messages as your phone is charging. Cut along the lines using an X-Acto knife. Keep the back of the newly created basket higher and cut a hole about the size of a socket. Spray paint the container or wrap in fabric using glue. Slide the plug into the hole and socket to attach to the wall.

bookshelves bonus

Although not a room or really a zone, bookshelves are both a necessary storage solution and a potential clutter collector. Rule number one: Don't double stack books.

And ask yourself the Three Bookshelf Qs:

1. Do I love it?
2. Do I read it?
3. Can I find this info online?

Classics can stay, but only if you actually reread or reference them. Clear out old travel guides and other reference tomes that simply gather dust. Group books that make the cut by subject and size. Filing them by color amps up the design-y feel of your shelving. Also, keep some open space—it doesn't look as cluttered. Another trick: Store coffee-table books horizontally to break up the lines and accessorize with sentimental items. If you can keep it tidy, consider using the books you don't need to access regularly as a side table in the living room or by the bed. Neatly stack them (hardcovers work best) to the height of the furniture arm or bed and top with a task lamp and vase of flowers.

"No furniture is so charming as books."
—SYDNEY SMITH

where to toss

OK, you now (hopefully) have an absolutely massive pile of things you're going to get rid of. But just because it's on your toss list doesn't mean it should go straight to the Dumpster. There are some things that can live on without you.

Give it a new home

As the saying goes, one man's trash is another man's treasure. And just because your violin hasn't been played since your sophomore year doesn't mean someone else can't make beautiful music.

Yard Sales. Everything can be sold at a stoop sale or yard sale. Make sure the items are clean and in good-working order. Coordinate with neighbors to get a bigger reach and diversity of offerings.

Big Ticket Items. Craigslist and eBay are great sources for big ticket items. Craigslist is also perfect for selling (or just getting someone to haul off) furniture like sofas and mattresses, which because of the bed bug epidemic in recent years in most major metropolitan areas can no longer be accepted by many non-profit organizations. Scour the sites for competitive pricing, and post items with good-quality photos.

Clothes. Old clothes can be sold or donated. Buffalo Exchange, a recycle boutique, has a number of outposts across the country. The stores buy gently worn, current styles of clothing and accessories and consign higher-priced items, on occasion. Many resale shops consign as well. The terms of acceptance vary at each local consignment shop, as do the fee structures. If you have a load of gently worn designer pieces, explore The RealReal. This online, members-only resale boutique employs fashion editors to assess and curate a selection of vintage goodies. If you're looking simply to donate (and get a tax credit), drop off clean clothes to your local Salvation Army, Goodwill, or church thrift shop. These places also accept any

GARBAGE BY THE NUMBERS

- The Garbage Path, aka Garbage Island, a collection of trash floating in the Pacific Ocean is believed to be the twice the size of Texas.
- Americans produce 50 million tons of electronic gadget waste a year. Only about 20% of that is properly recycled according to The Earth Day Network. See "Where to Toss" on page 41 for how to dispose of your electronics the right way.
- The average person produces 4.3 pounds of waste daily, according to the Duke Center for Sustainability & Commerce.
- About 34 millions tons of food is wasted annually. Less than 3% was recycled in 2009, according to research

other kind of working household items, as well as books, music, and magazines. Another possibility is specialized donation drives: Donatemydress.org for prom and special occasion frocks; Dress for Success is all about work- and interview-appropriate clothing and unopened makeup for women; One Warm Coat is a national coat drive initiative.

Outdated Electronics. Old technology can be recycled at retailers like Apple, Staples, and Best Buy. Gazelle.com buys used gadgets of all kinds. Donate your used cell phone at any Verizon location for their HopeLine program, which helps victims of domestic violence. Or give it to Cell Phones for Soldiers, a non-profit for active-duty military families and veterans.

conducted at Duke. See "Three Steps to Compost at Home" on page 62 for compost tips.

- The United States has more than 3,500 landfills.
- More than 7 billion pounds of PVC (the most common plastic) is tossed each year in the U.S., reports earth911. org.
- Americans use 1 billion—yes that's a "b"—plastic bags a year.
- Each year, 360 million pairs of shoes are trashed to U.S. landfills.
- Paper and packaging materials account for approximately 30% of the waste sent to American landfills.
- There are between 6 and 15 million hoarders living in the United States.

Housewares and linens. Housewares are best donated to Goodwill centers, Freecycle, or posted on Craigslist. Donate old, clean linens to animal shelters. They'll take slightly torn sheets, blankets, and towels that otherwise can't be donated.

Magazines, books, and other media. Magazines, books, and other media can find new homes at thrift stores, nursing homes, and family shelters.

Beauty Products. Unused beauty products are welcome at any women's shelter or Beauty Bus, a non-profit that creates pop-up salons in the homes of women and men who are homebound due to illness.

Freecycle. For some items, consider joining the Freecycle Network. Just as the name indicates, this non-profit organization is an online match system for your old stuff and someone nearby who wants it. The system works vice versa, so if you're on the hunt for a TV stand, this may be a place to look. Donations are tax deductible.

Hauling services. More appropriate for total house cleanouts, 1-800-GOT-JUNK, a full-service disposal company, removes furnishings, unwieldy housewares and, you guessed it—junk—for a fee.

Swap your stuff: Three steps to host a swap party

Get rid of your stuff with a regifting fête.

1. **The prep.** An even amount of guests is ideal. Create a balance of items, styles, sizes, and personalities. Put instructions on the invite as to what you'd like guests

to bring (clothes, housewares, books, or just one category) and the condition—clean, gently worn, or new, for example. Also set a minimum and maximum number of items. The goal is to get rid of stuff, not accumulate more.

2. **The party.** Serve classic snacks and appetizers. See recipes starting on page 148 in Part Three for ideas. Have each guest do a show and tell with the items they brought. Anyone who is interested raises a hand. Pieces that have more than one taker get put into a "fight" pile. When show and tell concludes, take out the fight pile. Have guests try on those items in question or make their case for why they need it, and have impartial partygoers decide who is better fit for the selection.

3. **The clean-up.** Have an immediate donation strategy. Anything that isn't taken should be removed from your home at the end of the party. Remember, this is a strategy to get rid of clutter!

sentimental items

Take a deep breath. Although it may seem like the hardest part of your purge process, it's also going to be the biggest space saver. First, remember your house is not your very own Graceland. Your home is a functional retreat that reflects your personality, not a place that pays homage to your past. So clear out those ballet shoes, that trumpet sheet music, and all the kindergarten self-portraits, and invite your current life in. You may feel some obligation to hold onto the tea set from Aunt Margie or tool chest from Grandpa Steve, but if it doesn't suit your lifestyle, it's nothing more than a dust collector. Use the Three Sentimental Qs to assess your extra special and—let's face it—not so special things.

1. **What does it say about you?** A majority of our sentimental clutter doesn't necessarily serve a purpose. If you hold onto things of memory, they should, like all of your things, be functional. If the purpose is no longer valid—your high school prom dress or your stuffed pal, Teddy—it's heading toward the dustbin. However, certain items that define you or your experiences deserve a second look. One thought as you shuffle through your belongings: how the cast of *CSI* would classify you. Would they say you are a pack-rat who holds onto old mail? Or could they call you

a romantic who valued a collection of love letters? Translation: You've got to prioritize your stuff.

Be sure to touch each item. And go with your gut. Anything that gives you warm fuzzies can go into a Keep pile. If you feel a bit *eh* about your collection of notes from the 5th grade, place it in the Not Sure pile. Go back to them. Still feeling *mezza*? Place them in a labeled box. When you do your next quarterly purge and you haven't taken a look at the insides, it's adios o'clock. If you really need a physical record of your crush on Tommy Brady, select the best of the collection and toss the rest.

Acknowledge that heirlooms need some extra attention. If Grandmother's silver and your great-grandpa's pipe from his crossing don't suit your lifestyle, store them in a safe place, or consider trading with a family member for something that's more your jam.

2. **Can it be digitized?** It doesn't take a PhD in spatial relationships to figure out that a single computer takes up less space than a pile of videos, photo albums, CDs, and other stuff. Compact your media onto your laptop, and scan photos or important letters. Some organization bloggers swear by digital scrapbooks composed of images of formerly favored items—concert ticket stubs, Mickey Mouse ears, shot glasses from your Vegas visit—that you've now recycled (see "Storage Solutions" on page 49 for giving your things a new home). If the item—a

sweater, stuffed puppy, or sofa, for example—can't be digitized, ask yourself where it will live. Remember: Everything needs a specific home in your small space.

3. **Would you bring it to a desert island?** We've all got that totally frivolous item that we'd bring on a trek to the *Blue Lagoon* (and ladies, waterproof mascara doesn't count—it's totally necessary!). If your dog-eared copy of *Winnie the Pooh* makes the list, it stays. These items should be proudly displayed.

storage solutions

Now that you've whittled down what you need to the bare essentials and the things that make you happy, it's time to figure out the best places for everything to live. Leave no surface unexplored for new possibilities, no empty container unconsidered for its storage value.

Clever reuse

Ask any politician, image is all about the packaging. Re-imagine common household items into serious storage MVPs:

- Stash unruly plastic bags in a vacant tissue box or paper towel roll. Plastic antibacterial wipe containers are another great option.
- Store your camera in a waterproof travel soap tray. Crafting needs and hair accessories also fit well in the inexpensive, plastic-covered trays.
- Thoroughly wash out tuna cans, then place them in a junk drawer, under the bathroom sink, or on the top of your desk to contain errant odds and ends that have no classification but are important enough to keep.
- Use a towel rack to hang cleaning products with trigger handles.

- House shoes in an old wine box. Turn the box on its side and slide your shoes into each compartment. Wrap the box in fabric affixed with ModgePodge (available at craft stores) to give it a more design-y look.

- Dryer sheets are reuse superstars. Use one as a lint remover, a computer screen duster, or an iron soleplate degunker. Toss one in your vacuum bag or line drawers with eco-friendly sheets for a fresh scent.

- You cook exactly 15 times a year so who can blame you that you don't have a trivet? A mouse pad works just as well. Just make sure it doesn't have a plastic coating, which can melt off when touched by a hot pan.

- Expensive shoes and bags often come with a dust bag, a cloth sack that protects soles from closet wear and ensures the bottoms won't soil anything else. A shower cap wrapped around a pair of shoes does the same thing.

- A vintage (or new) picture frame makes a perfect drinks tray. Place a solid piece of paper in the frame. It'll look more functional and less repurposed. Or line it with old hotel key cards for a cool conversational piece.

- Stack bangles around a lone candlestick. Choose one with a deep reservoir area; it can be used as a bud vase. Cut the stem down so the flower won't topple over.

- Cut pieces of corkboard into four-inch squares. It's a fashionable and quickie way to make coasters.
- Place a bento box on your desk to corral office supplies like paper clips, Post-It notes, and iPod chargers. Use the compartmentalized containers to organize your fantasy football stats and different team info. Or refashion a bento box as a jewelry caddy. The multiple compartments can house your earrings, bracelets, and necklaces.
- Place a napkin holder on your landing strip (page 14) to serve as a mail collector. Dish drying racks make great file organizers. Choose one in brushed metal for an urban design touch.
- An accordion-style wooden wine rack is a clever way to stow a few towels. Roll them up and slide into the slots.
- In the bathroom, a silver-plated mint julep cup is just the right height to hold makeup brushes, disposable razors, and toothbrushes. Cleaned-out Diptyque candle glasses work just as well; the graphic labels look chic in any space.

Think vertically

Besides being about virtually nothing, one of the hallmarks of the '90s comedy phenom *Seinfeld* was the bike hanging from the ceiling in the apartment of the namesake character. Copy that idea. It's a good one. Hang oversize sporting items such as the aforementioned bike or your skis close to the ceiling. Also go up with any shelving units you may bring in. Store things that you won't need daily, such as seasonal items like your Christmas decorations or your BBQ necessities in attractive containers. Not only do streamlined, vertical storage spaces declutter the floor, they also help your place look bigger. It's a trick on the eye—having storage solutions up draws the focus toward the ceiling.

Use the doors

The key to living large in a shoebox is to utilize all available areas, and the back of your doors are the epitome of such spaces. The Container Store specializes in all things Type-A organization, and carries a host of back-of-the-door solutions from baskets to hooks. (As does Amazon.) If you're a crafter, place your gear in baskets lined along the inside of your closet door. Store gym equipment, knitting yarns, and wrapping needs in over-the-door shoe hangers. Of course, you can use a shoe holder for its actual function, but many prefer to store soles on shelves in the closets, or in stacked clear plastic boxes. In the bathroom, maximize cabinet doors by affixing mini holders (like the ones used inside high school lockers) for Q-tips and your toothbrush. Magnetic spice racks also do the trick. In the office, affix a clear folder to the back of a door and fill with important papers that require quick access.

See it

Out of sight, out of mind. And never is that more true than in organization. If your stuff is crammed into drawers and

THREE QUESTIONS FOR SHOPPING

Now that you've uncluttered, you want to keep it that way. Think before you buy, and abide by the In/Out Rule. The concept is simple: For everything you bring into your home and closet, you've got to ditch one comparable item. It's pretty self-explanatory—buy a new sweater, toss an old one. Expand on the idea and weigh space versus cost when making purchases. Good deals aren't so good when you don't have an inch to store yet another pair of jeans. You may also want to institute a 48-hour wait period before buying so you can figure out what is going to get tossed before you purchase whatever it is you have your eye on.

For clothes:

1. Does this fit me well?
2. Does it vibe with the other items in my closet?
3. Will I wear it more than once?

For gadgets:

1. What is its function?
2. How often am I going to use it?
3. Do I own something that does essentially the same thing?

For furniture:

1. What is its function?
2. Does it coordinate with my vision and current décor?
3. What are the cleaning and fabric-care instructions?

For home accessories:

1. What does it say about me?
2. Where is it going to live?
3. Does it coordinate with my vision and current décor?

packed into your closet, you're less likely to see it, which means you won't often use it. And if you don't use it, you lose it. Create storage areas where items are recognizable in three seconds flat. Employ stacking shelves, see-through containers, and labels to make things easily accessible.

Repeat: Baskets and trays

Baskets and trays. Containment is key. Make a home for your linens in a large weaved hamper. Create a bin for gloves and scarves, and toss magazines in structured crates placed by the couch. Trays create the perfect enclosed area for top-of-the-vanity items in the bathroom, decorative pieces and errant grooming products that are used too often to be stored in drawers.

Dress up the furniture

A skirted table, bed, or sink has a little secret. It's hiding not-oft-used stuff in a pretty way. Repurpose a shower curtain or take an old curtain and adhere it to the sink or open shelving unit using Velcro or multi-purpose glue. Choose a bold graphic print that won't show dirt or use. In the bedroom, dress up a nightstand to house bags or shoes below; conceal crafting needs, wrapping supplies, and media under the TV.

Add an entry

It may seem counterintuitive to take up space directly at the door, but it's actually a space saver. Just like the landing strips (page 14), the entryway is a dedicated space for items you always use. Place a bookshelf by your entrance and store shopping bags, shoes, umbrellas, and mittens. Leave a dish for keys and outgoing mail. Or affix some hooks (vintage ones look fashionable) to the wall to hang coats, canvas bags, and more. Having an on-the-go zone streamlines your entire home.

Create a utility closet

Errant brooms, Swiffers, and other household products create a clunky, cluttered mess. Cordon off an area in your closet that's specifically dedicated to containing cleaning products, tools, and laundry supplies. Affix hanging clips to the wall, freeing up floor space for boots or gardening supplies.

clean green

Make room under your sink for more shoes or your climbing equipment by going green on the clean scene. Swap out the endless oversize bottles of harsh chemicals for a host of everyday kitchen grime-ridders like baking soda and white vinegar.

Three items that you should keep in your arsenal are a wet Swiffer (place an old T-shirt over the pad to dust); a handheld vacuum, like a Dust Buster; and antibacterial wipes, which can spot clean any surface in a jiffy. Opt for the ones in an envelope—they take up less storage space.

While you're getting all down with Mother Earth, keep foldable shopping bags on hand. Store them on the hooks affixed to the back of the cabinet doors and always keep one in your car or purse. Baggu has a host of stowable, washable offerings in cute colors and styles.

DIY clean

Baking soda. The ultimate powerhouse when it comes to clean, this little miracle worker can polish everything from teeth to your tub. Leave an open box in your fridge or on the countertop to absorb odors. Tuck it by the stove so your entire apartment doesn't smell like last night's dinner. Before vacuuming, sprinkle it on your rugs—it'll remove pet odors. To clean pots, mix with a bit of dishwashing soap (just avoid using on aluminum, as it can tarnish). Use that same paste to scrub your tub. Add a drop or two of your favorite essential oil for an antibacterial boost and a less medical scent. See "Decoding Scents" on page 171.

White vinegar. Packed with antimicrobial properties, vinegar kills mold, bacteria, even weeds. Dilute with water in a 1-1 ratio and spritz straight onto bathroom tiles and grout. Let it sit for 15 minutes, before scrubbing. Perk up dingy silver by soaking in a mix of ½ cup of white vinegar with three tablespoons of baking soda for two hours. Rinse with cold water and dry thoroughly.

GREEN WORDS

Downcycle. First used in the early '90s, this process converts useless products or waste into new materials of lesser quality. For example, when plastics are recycled to lower grade ones.

Precycle. The practice of reducing garbage by purchasing items that generate less waste.

Recycle. A synonym for downcycle. The aim of recycling is to reduce waste by melting and reusing it to create an inferior-quality product to the original.

Reuse. A two-pronged practice where items are either refashioned for a new use or conventionally reused for the same original function.

Upcycle. The opposite of downcycling, the term refers to the practice of converting waste or useless products into new materials of superior quality. The process commonly results in textiles.

Lemon. Polish wood with two parts olive oil and one part lemon juice. Similarly, a gallon of water with four table-spoons of lemon juice can effectively clean mirrors. A cloth dipped in straight lemon juice can remove stains on vinyl. After you've used the juice, you can utilize the citrus half as a sponge for the sink or your fingernails.

Salt. Remove water and heat rings on your favorite wood table with a thin paste made of salt, lemon juice, and oil. Place on the effected area and lightly buff away using a cloth. Polish metals with salt diluted in vinegar. Add a dash of lemon for brass fixtures.

Aspirin. Toss the headache reliever into the washing machine to brighten whites.

Rubbing alcohol. Use a water-diluted blend to clean mirrors and windows and other reflective services. Witch hazel works as well.

room-by-room storage solutions

Bedroom

BUILD OUT THE CLOSETS

The easiest way to expand your storage space is to customize it. Sweaters, pants, skirts, and shoes get more breathing room when a closet is more than a single hanging bar. The Container Store has a host of solutions that you can use to tweak spaces for your specific needs, with installation service. Ikea also sells closet modular systems, as do Amazon and Bed, Bath & Beyond. Also, think about shoe and bag storage. Does it need to be in the closet? Or would you rather house your collection of Adidas in a more artful manner? Once you've built out your closet space—don't forget to utilize the doors—opt for huggable hangers. They occupy less space than the plastic ones and are more streamlined than wire hangers you got from the dry cleaners.

ACCESSORIZE

Invest in décor pieces that are more than just pretty faces. Antique glove molds make fantastic storage/display sites for necklaces and other jewelry. Place a selection of glass cylinders of various heights and widths on the windowsill. In them, catch accessories, colorful scarves, reclaimed hardware, or any other little thing you like collecting. Or hang a corkboard for storage of similar items, as well as baseball caps, belts, and ties (affix hooks so they don't wrinkle). Chic-ify the look and cover the cork with a favorite image blown up in black-and-white.

CUSTOMIZE A CLOSET

Create your own closet. Eschew the store-bought kits for a personalized closet fashioned with plywood, cut into 16-inch wide pieces. Measure and cut down into smaller pieces as needed, making sure sections are evenly matched to create boxes and shelves. Secure boxes to each other with screws. Then secure to the wall (use drywall anchors for a more sturdy finish). Drill holes for the rods, which should be approximately 11.5 inches from the back wall.

Sectioned off. To add insult to injury, it's very common for small spaces to be completely closet-free. Portion out a storage section in either a corner or long wall area. Note: Bump out the measurements by a few inches to hang a curtain or doors to the system. Then hang a modular system connected to a flat wall or a personalized one (see above).

Hanging system. This is the cheapest and easiest system to implement. Select a corner to house the rod and cut a wooden dowel to size. Screw two crown bolt hooks into the ceiling. Loop twine into the hooks and securely around the rod. And there you have it—an insta-storage area.

MAKE THE BED

A made bed makes everything appear that much more pulled together. Happiness bonus: Studies show that people who make their beds in the morning are more productive. See "Three Steps to Make the Bed—Properly" on page 103 for tips on dressing your bed hotel-style.

DIY OLD-SCHOOL SOLUTION

Murphy Bed: Build the bed box using medium-density fiberboard or plywood as the base. Frame around the mattress with 1" x 12" boards cut to snugly fit. Use nails to secure. At the pivot point, screw in hinges. Position the Murphy bed on its side and utilize the surface as a credenza. Paint or wallpaper the plywood to seamlessly blend with your home's décor. Position bookcases around the bed to camouflage it further.

Kitchen

CLEAR THE COUNTER

A gadget-free counter space can make a tiny kitchen look a bit bigger (as can a glass-tiled backsplash). Ditch the mondo coffee maker for a French press instead. The small strainer-like mechanism can also steep tea, froth milk, infuse oils, and assist in making baby food. Consider swapping out a dish rack with an ultra-absorbent kitchen cloth that can easily be stashed away when guests come.

DECANT

Stop the avalanche of dry goods and invest in sets of canisters. Remove packaged foods, rice, and pasta from their original wrappers and store in glass containers with lids. The jars should be uniform in style and stacking abilities. Consider labeling them to ease the what-are-you guessing game. Anthropologie, Target, and Pier 1 Imports sell wide-mouth jars with chalkboard labels.

TAKE OFF THE DOORS

It may seem a bit counterintuitive when you want to hide your mess. But removing the cabinet doors can actually keep you organized. Neatly stack plates and glasses, and line the lower shelves with your glass food canisters. Paint the inside of the cabinets the same color as your walls to give the illusion of a wider area.

THREE STEPS TO COMPOST AT HOME

1. Place an aerated bucket (Williams-Sonoma sells them) under the sink. An old, covered coffee can works just as well. Cut a few holes in the bottom and plastic top. Place a dish below the can.
2. Add a bit of soil and shredded newspaper to the bottom of the can. Place food scraps on top. Turn over once a week to aid in decomposition.
3. Once the components are no longer identifiable, use the compost as fertilizer in your plants. Or recycle at your local farmers' market.

Living room and office

MOUNT IT

Streamline your space and eliminate the need for an extra piece of furniture by mounting your desk on the wall. Design Within Reach, CB2, and Ikea all carry some great floating desk options. Choose a style with a flip-out drawer for a quick declutter trick. If you're hesitant to drill something so permanent to the wall, choose a storage system (bookcase or cubby arrangement) with a functional surface space for a laptop and other desk needs.

RING THE CEILING

Amplify the ceiling height and draw the eye up with books stored by the ceiling. Hang a shelf about 20 inches from the ceiling or rest above the door's high sash or window frame. To limit the appearance of clutter, line the shelf with books according to size and color. Affix a string of LED lights to the shelf if the space looks too dark.

CREATE COFFEE-TABLE STORAGE

Slide baskets under your sofa side table to contain clutter. Measure the space from the floor to the bottom of the table and invest in two baskets that can easily slide in and out of that area. In them, place your extra throws (more than one on the back of your couch can look messy), magazines, and remote controls.

Bathroom

BE CADDY

Harness all your grooming products (including razors, makeup brushes, and the hair dryer) into a plastic cleaning caddy. Under the sink, use stepped shelf organizers to create more storage space. Store makeup, Q-Tips, and cotton balls in divided silverware trays. Place any product doubles in a tackle box and label with masking tape.

SWING

Hang a three-tiered fruit basket from the ceiling above the tub. Fill with face washes, loofahs, and other bath accessories. Place it in the corner.

USE A WINE CRATE

Scour your local flea market for vintage wooden boxes, which are the perfect size for storing towels. Turn it on the high side, and utilize it as a side table for a surface. Inside, stack rolled towels. Place fresh flowers, your toothbrush, and soap on the top. Contain any accessories in a tray or an open jewelry box.

PART TWO:
DÉCOR

"Beauty of style and harmony and grace and
good rhythm depend on simplicity."
—PLATO

more is less—sort of

Unlike putting lipstick on a pig, how you dress, decorate, and furnish your shoebox has a huge effect on not only appearance and feeling, but also function. Color, furniture selection, and accessory placement can make your living space appear bigger. Yes, it's true! As you learned in the first section of this guide, how you use each square inch and each item in your home is key to living large in a small space.

Play it straight

Overstuffed furniture can make a small space look, well, overstuffed. Larger pieces will work better if they have sleek lines and muted colors. Bold prints appear not only dated but also way bigger than they actually are. Since the largest piece of furniture sets the pace and scale for the rest of your place, make sure it isn't overpowering. You know that sectional that you've got to crawl over to get to the phone/bathroom/anything else in your apartment? Yeah, um, it's not working. See "Where to Toss" on page 41 for donation suggestions. Opt for low-slung sofas and chairs, which can appear less dense. Also, go for gams. Choose couches and other stuffed pieces that show their legs. Draped or covered furniture legs mask the floor, making your space seem smaller.

COUCHED BY THE NUMBERS

Full-size: The most common sofa style measures more than 78 inches wide, but generally no more than 84 inches, and usually has three full cushions.

Apartment sofa: Measures anywhere from 66 to 77 inches wide and is no more than 40 inches deep. Arms are smaller and there are usually two cushions.

Love seat: Consists of two cushions and is shaped more like its full-size counterparts (with high arms). Generally measure 58 to 60 inches wide and 35 inches deep.

Sleeper sofa: Also called a sofa bed, this generally measures 70 inches wide and about 90 inches when fully extended. Queen-size sofa sleepers are about 84 inches wide and the standard 90 inches open. Some can be as long as 109 inches. Twin sizes (54 inches wide, 85 inches open) are less common.

Futon: The classic bi-fold futon is available in queen and full. The more common of the two, the full measures 75 inches wide (without arms) and is 54 inches extended. The queen is bigger at 80 inches by 42 inches.

Map it out

Take out a piece of graph paper. (It will be easier to see spatial proportions.) On it, sketch out your space looking from above. Mark out the doors and windows. Fashion Post-It notes or pieces of construction paper as furniture tokens. Move them around the apartment blueprint to get an idea of your space's best layout. During this exercise you'll also want to keep the number three in your mind. Design experts agree three feet is the optimal space for passageways (where two or more people need to go by each other), getting in and out of chairs, and opening drawers. In other words, it's the x-factor for flow. If you can't eke out three feet for your dresser drawers, choose an alternative storage solution. For example, a repurposed bookcase or a curio cabinet can house your sweaters while giving you space to move around. But keep in mind your vision of space from page 6 to keep things cohesive. Also think about how you'll incorporate your personality and sentimental items when you sketch the layout of your home.

Focus

Avoid the temptation to fill your home with multiple mini furnishings. While you may feel like the small stature will work in your space, in reality, it will end up just looking cluttered. Instead the key is creating a single focal point. Dress your room around the largest items in the room—your antique armoire, the double Ikea Billy bookcase, and your day bed. Place the large pieces in strategic spots to draw the eye to the special characteristics of your room. Consider situating the couch on a diagonal to elongate the visual space or use bookshelves to separate a workspace from the living area. See page 69 for more space divider tips.

If you're without one main stage furnishing, consider using a large piece of art to achieve the same effect. A conversation piece on the wall also can also alter the space

FIND ZEN

Minimalism is a tenant of Zen, the Buddhist offshoot that seeks complete and absolute peace of mind and body through simplicity.

1. Continue to eliminate physical clutter from your home. Ensure everything has an assigned place.
2. Choose solid, simple, functional furnishings.
3. Select a muted color palette.
4. Utilize comfortable flooring.
5. Place your bed next to a natural light source.
6. Enhance your space with calming, natural scents. See "Decoding Scents" on page 171 for tips.
7. Place green plants around your home. See "Kill-proof Plants" on page 99 for tips on caring for plants.
8. Remove electronic excess.

relations since it draws the eye away from the populated floor. Another trick: Keep the floor rug-free. It creates the illusion of more space.

Divide and conquer

Chances are your small space is more like a single room, and you've got to divide that space into "rooms" to create a living room, dining room, office, and possibly bedroom. Delineating your shoebox into distinct and functional areas makes organization easier and can help life be a little more Zen. See "Find Zen" above for tips on getting Zen.

MAKE A FURNITURE FRONTIER LINE

A console table behind the sofa can be used as a desk, which can separate the bed from the public area of your apartment. Strategically placed bookcases also do the trick. A light-reflecting credenza or even a TV console can mark the separation between the room's distinct uses. By performing double duty, these types of room dividers won't take up too much floor space. If you're low on closet space, this is a great way to introduce a wardrobe—use it as a frontier line. See "Customize a Closet" on page 60 for closet-making tips.

USE RUGS AS BORDER CONTROL

Instead of positioning furniture in the middle of the room, literally place a line in the sand with floor coverings. Place a remnant of carpet under your desk or extend a runner across the foot of your bed to mark the separate areas. The different treatments will impart a distinct vibe to each area.

CREATE A WALL OF CURTAINS

Or use screens to physically demarcate the space. Choose shades or draperies that are translucent enough to allow the movement of natural light. Or tie back the curtains when the bedroom, for example, is not in use.

SPACE IT OUT

Simply place the bed on the other side of the room from the couch for a visual separation of space and its use. The key with this remedy is to give each major piece of furniture a spatial border of about seven feet from the other.

Open up

Your instinct to place all your furniture along the walls is the wrong one. Lining up furnishings can actually create a crowded sense. Instead, float pieces away from the wall in groupings. Creating clearance away from the walls creates the illusion of more space. Again, the magic number is three. Gather your sofa, coffee table, and a credenza, for example. Use a bench or your couch as a bed footboard and set a coffee table nearby. Or set up a desk space with a chair and oversize floor lamp together. To ensure flow, keep passage areas free.

So cozy

Home is where the heart is. It's a place of security, comfort, and warmth. And sometimes you and your design sense are a bit more cocoon-like than sleek and open. It's actually easier to make your small space cozy as opposed to bigger. So, you may as well embrace it. Deep saturated colors on the walls or furnishings, heavy fabric draperies, and ornate rugs can all do that. Dark woods and animal prints are more coziness makers. Of course, you don't want your place to look too much like a vampire's lair, so keep your place well-lit. And it should still be clutter-free. Being packed to the gills just makes cozy look messy and a bit like Miss Havisham lives here.

dos and don'ts: shopping for second-hand furniture

Vintage furnishings are a great way to introduce personality to your place on a budget. Purchasing second-hand furniture is also earth-friendly. Since merchandise changes daily, make regular visits to your local flea markets, thrift stores, and consignment shops. Apartment therapy.com has a handy weekly roundup of Craigslist picks. Use eBay alerts for keeping up with new postings. Note: To be considered vintage, pieces must be at least 30 years old. Antiques are 100 or older.

Do: Inspect

Do both a visual and a physical inspection once (or twice) over. Take a look at the materials and quality of the piece in question. Do the drawers open and close easily? Is the wood or veneer even and not warped? Also, carefully examine the upholstery for tears, marks, and odors. Certain fabric styles are easy to fix (covering benches and tacked-on cushions just need a new swatch and a glue gun); others require a pro. Vintage plastic cushions should be pliable and not cracked. Don't forget to take a seat. Test furniture for comfort as well as function.

Do: Look at the inner beauty

Choose high-quality, functional items with good bones. Look beyond the ugly colors and rusted accents. Those cosmetic accents can easily be changed to complement your design sense. Richly pigmented paint like that from Valspar does wonders to wake up a piece. And switching out hardware is an inexpensive way to make your purchase look more

ONLINE VINTAGE FURNITURE SOURCES

eBay. The big daddy of online sellers, this auction-site is a bonanza of all things pre-owned. Tip: Search for misspelled brand names.

Etsy. Individual sellers are showcased at a single source. Best bets include design details and accent pieces.

Craigslist. The Classifieds of the Internet age, the listing service offers an array of cash-and-carry furnishing options.

One Kings Lane. This free, membership-only sale site showcases tightly curated selections based around design themes and lifestyle needs. Sister site Joss & Main is a similar concept.

Goodwill. Operated by the charity organization, shopgoodwill .com auctions an edited selection from shops across the country.

GovDeals. A warehouse of government-confiscated items, this site sells furniture and fine art next to office equipment and cars and other machinery.

modern. Similarly, repurpose items to fit your needs. Use a vintage bar cart as a TV console, store shoes in a bookcase, or fashion a bedside table out of a high-back chair.

Do: Measure

Imagine the major bummer if your new-to-you-score-of-the-century has to stay on the stoop because it doesn't fit through your front door. Keep measurement notes in your phone. Note the height, width, and diagonal width of your passageways and door openings. Make sure you measure inside the doorframe from bottom right to top left. In order to maneuver it well, furniture should be at least four inches smaller than your hallway. See "Steps to Measure a Room" on page 24 for tips.

Don't: Hesitate

Here today, gone tomorrow. Never was such an adage so true as when shopping for vintage. Stock is generally limited to single pieces. If you like something and it fits your needs and budget, pull the trigger and purchase.

Don't: Buy to buy

A good deal is only good if you need the item. Don't get swept up in the $30 price tag. If the piece doesn't work in your home or doesn't have a function, it's no longer a deal. See the Three Furniture Qs on page 22 for shopping tips.

Don't: Go repro

With the industrial, patina-look doing gangbusters these days among the interior design set, there's a plethora of fakes. Manufactured in Asia, these pieces are lighter and less sturdy than their vintage counterparts. If quality and durability are a priority, look for a maker's mark or seal on the bottom.

Bargain bonus: How to haggle

Everything is negotiable, especially at flea markets, estate sales, antique stores, and on Craigslist.

SIMPLY ASK

If items aren't marked, the prices aren't set in stone. Ask the seller for her best number. Or begin the haggle yourself. It's a good idea to ask for a discount of ⅓ off the quoted price, and bargain from there.

NOTE THE CONDITION

If an item is chipped or scratched, you're more likely to get a discount than if it is in perfect condition. Use that as your negotiating point.

MAKE MULTIPLE PURCHASES

A group buy means more merchandise is moving out, and that's often grounds for a lower price on the total.

FOLLOW THE RULES

Many antique stores post pricing guidelines. If there's a firm stance, don't push the issue.

go double duty

No surprises here—multipurpose furnishings are serious space savers. Ikea and CB2 sell headboards with shelving, as does Pottery Barn. Store seasonal items and guest linens in a vintage chest, then use it closed as a coffee- or bedside table. Place a cushion on top of a horizontal Ikea Lack shelf *et voilà*, you've got a bench. The shelving unit can also be utilized as a TV console and room divider. Vintage filing cabinets can house more than paperwork. And of course, the sofa sleeper and the stow ottomans are the ultimate apartment-friendly pieces, as are daybeds with trundles.

DIY STORAGE BEDS

Platform storage bed: Create a frame the same size as your mattress with a series of rectangular storage cubbies. Screw a series of plywood slats across the cubes to secure them to each other and reinforce the base. Add a solid piece of plywood over the criss-crossed slats. Secure with screws.

Bookcase headboard: Start with an assembled standard bookcase. Place the bed against the wall. Center the bookcase horizontally over the bed. Screw the shelving unit into the wall. Make sure everything is properly secured to the studs with cleats. Embellish with wallpaper or paint. Storage cubes and floating shelves can also be used.

make it mobile

By making furniture easy to move, you can make it work for you in a ton of scenarios.

Put it on wheels

We've talked a lot about flow—it's the balance, the energy, and feeling of the home. It's also the blueprint for how people move physically and visually throughout your home. So it stands to reason that having furnishings that are easy to shuffle can improve the flow. Put a console on wheels and it can be shifted to the corner and set up as a bar for your annual champagne party. A wheelie nightstand can be repositioned as a side table. A bed on casters or a coffee table on skates can also be moved with little effort. Bonus: Cleaning the floor is a snap. Casters are easy to attach to the bottom of furniture. Fixed wheels move in a single direction; swivels are true to their name. Screw the wheels to heavier pieces, as light chairs tend to move on their own. Also, when not on the move, place wheels in caster cups, available at Sears and Amazon.

Fold it away

Rolling with the furniture on wheels concept, choose furnishings that can be moved, folded, or repurposed in a snap. Folding kitchen islands create more prep space and can double as a serving station at dinner parties. Drop-leaf dining tables can easily be expanded for dinner parties, then contracted and used as a console. Nesting tables are the perfect solution to extra surface area, and good old-fashioned folding chairs invite guests to take a seat. Tuck folded chairs under the bed or alongside the fridge when not in use. Floor pillows (available at Urban Outfitters, West Elm, and Bed, Bath & Beyond) can also create more seating. Or introduce poufs. Originally from North Africa, the collapsible stools come in a variety of colors and fabrics. Check Etsy and Fab.com for options.

lighten up

Watch HGTV and you'll see designers embracing wall color. While it definitely infuses personality to a space, it can also make it appear cozier. Dark hues absorb light, thus making a room seem smaller. Instead of going deep, choose creamy-infused, neutral colors in cooler tones. In addition to showcasing your home's natural light, such colors also create the illusion of more space. If white walls are too clinical, opt for icy blues, tawny-toned neutrals, pale yellows, cool greens, and muted grays. Complement walls with trim work painted in lighter colors. The effect is a roomier, airier space. Similarly, painting large furniture pieces—armoires or chests of drawers—the same color as the walls can widen out the room. Painting the inside of a bookcase or storage cube also imparts such an illusion.

Let there be light

Fact: Any room appears larger with the sun streaming in. So much so that natural light visually expands exponentially compared to other tricks. Keep your windows wide open—visually—allowing light to come in. If you've got a less than million dollar view, place natural elements like a terrarium or flowers on the sill. You'll camouflage the ugly while still celebrating the natural. For more tips on plants see "Kill-proof Plants" on page 99.

Is your apartment north-facing, or are you relegated to a basement level? Use lighting to enhance the illusion of space. Skip the single overhead light. And ditch anything that gives off a brash department-store feel. Swap out on-and-off only switches for dimmers on ceiling lights—recessed systems and chandeliers work best. Scatter soft-lit lamps around your space. Situate them about 18 inches from the wall to create the illusion of depth. And space them about three feet from each other—this will allow the light to bounce across the walls, again playing a spatial visual trick. In the kitchen, affix under-cabinet lighting to refresh the space. Pink bulbs impart a soft glow.

FIFTY SHADES OF NEUTRAL

A rose by any other name would smell as sweet. Synonyms for basic colors:

Beige: biscuit, buff, café au lait, camel, cream, ecru, fawn, khaki, mushroom, natural, neutral, oatmeal, off-white, sand, tan, taupe

Gray: ash, ashen, charcoal, dove, granite, gunmetal, heather, oyster, powder, silvered, slate, stone

White: alabaster, antique, chalk, cornsilk, lace, lily, linen, milk, ivory, opal, paper, pearl, seashell, snow

Yellow: amber, banana, blonde, canary, champagne, chiffon, citrine, golden, goldenrod, honey, lemon, saffron, straw, sunshine, topaz

Treat your windows

Although wide, open windows allow the most light, they can also have an unfinished look (not to mention the lack of privacy!). Dress windows with sheer drapes that allow the maximum amount of sunshine. Go for lightweight cotton, linen, or lace fabric as opposed to heavy canvas or velvet. And stick with solid colors and monochromatic designs, which maintain the illusion of depth. Tie back curtains during the day to allow the most amount of natural light to stream in. Amplify the effect even more by matching the curtains to the walls. Another visual trick: Hang your drapes wider and longer than the windows. It will elongate the illusion of the window, therefore psychologically inviting more light. If you simply hate the concept of drapes (hey, we get it, they can take up loads of surface space), opt for semi transparent shades made of materials such as rice paper that allow the maximum amount of light.

get on the floor

Just like Pepsi or Coke, Jennifer Aniston or Angelina Jolie, dawn or dusk, the question of light floors or dark ultimately comes down to personal taste. On one hand, we've got the basic, clean, and widening effect of natural, beige, and other neutral-toned flooring. On the other, the dark surfaces have a sophisticated and anchoring look that tend to leave a home looking "finished." Some also say a darker floor has a more homey feel. No matter which you choose, go for a uniform treatment of the color.

Go au naturel

Parquet looks dated and can confuse the cohesive look of the home. If opting for dark, it's best to stick with natural elements—wood, stone, concrete, cork—and true-to-life finishes in lieu of carpeting, which can be a bit overpowering and dense. Ikea, Home Depot, and Lumber Liquidators have wide selections of laminate wood-like flooring. Note: Dark floors need to be dusted more often.

Love the one you've got

If you can't change the flooring and you've got some old-school linoleum tiles that just won't get clean, spread out a rug. Although rugs tend to make a space look smaller, a clean floor is better than a shabby one. Choose a neutral-

ORIGINS OF "CARPET" AND "RUG"

Carpet: Middle English, from Middle French *carpite*, from Old Italian *carpita*, from *carpire* "to pluck," modification of Latin *carpere* "to pluck"

Rug: Middle English *rug rag, tuft,* probably of Scandinavian origin; akin to Norwegian dialect *rugga coarse rug*, Old Norse *rogg tuft*

colored rug to open up the space. Large prints can add an element of texture. If you're squeezed into a studio, opt for a monochromatic design or a tone-on-tone one. Rugs can also be used to delineate spaces. See "Divide and conquer" on page 69 for tips.

get reflective

Stop me if you've read this before: The key to creating a bigger feel is creating optical illusions. Glass tops, clear furnishings, and transparent surfaces are functional without weighing down a room. The real super stars in this department are mirrors and other reflective surfaces. Mirrors reflect light, making your space brighter and expanding the sense of depth.

Mirror, mirror, on which wall?

Place them on the walls and throughout your home to amplify the sense of space. Situate a large mirror near the window to invite more natural sunshine. For a dramatic effect, prop an oversize one against the wall. It will reflect a large part of the entire room and augment the proportions. Mirrored cabinet and closet doors have a similar effect. Energetically, mirrors are also positive. In the practice of feng shui they are often used to enhance *qi*. Place a mirror facing the entrance to your home to repel the entrance of negative energy, for example. To increase your chances of health and wealth, situate a mirror to reflect any plants, candles, or fireplaces. See page 86 for more feng shui tips.

MIRROR HISTORY: FUN FACTS

The Egyptians used mirrors. Venetians did too.

The first mirrors are believed to have been polished obsidian glass, which is sourced from volcanoes. The oldest remnants were found in what is now Turkey and date to 6,000 BCE.

Historians believe that Egyptians crafted ceramic bowls with the express purpose to fill with water and use as mirrors. A little later, in 4000 to 3000 BCE Mesopotamia, it is believed that polished copper was used as a reflective surface.

For many years, it was widely believed that mirrors were first invented by the Chinese during the late Shang Dynasty. They were fashioned from amalgams of silver and mercury.

During the Renaissance, a method similar to the Chinese was used until the 16th century in Venice, when a glass coating was introduced to the formula. Mirrors were still considered luxuries at the time.

In 1835, a German chemist invented silvered glass (essentially a coated glass), the precursor to modern-day mirrors. It allowed for mass production.

feng shui basics

Literally translated as "wind-water," the ancient Chinese practice of feng shui is the practice of object orientation to create the healthiest *qi* (pronounced chee), or energy flow. Recently, the concept of feng shui has melded into a concept of moving possessions around to create a positive energy balance and tangible results (e.g., better health, better luck, better job). While the practice is highly nuanced, there are a few quick tips to keep in mind before you begin organizing your space.

Every home is divided into nine categories. Each speaks to a different life situation. To enhance that section or corner of your life, certain colors and objects (think mirrors and plants) should occupy that space. Your entrance point serves as a baseline for the following chart:

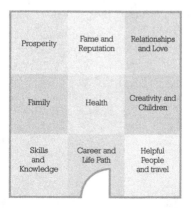

Career and life path. What is your calling in life? Do you have the best job for you? White and black help call upon the power of your life. Glass and mirrors serve as reflections as how the world sees you. Avoid earth-tone colors and square-shaped items here, which can muddy the path.

Helpful people and travel. In addition to being the area that helps call upon those who make your life easier (and happier), this section is also about being treated fairly. Silver, gray, and religious symbols invite assistance into your life. Placing a bell here signifies you want to be heard. Avoid having your garbage pail or landing strips (page 14) here, as they can suck away positive influences.

Creativity and children. Some feng shui experts suggest tackling this area of your home first, as it is the birthplace to new concepts and inspired ideas. White, yellow, and cylindrical-shaped objects invite imagination. Fire and the colors associated with it are a no-no here.

Relationships and love. To ensure harmony with others, this area must be balanced at all times. Candles, fresh flowers, and mirrors draw positive love and energy. Placing a storage unit here invites a relationship filled with unneeded baggage.

Fame and reputation. Easy, Lady Gaga, this isn't about you ruling the world in a meat dress, it's about how the world sees you. It's about your integrity and honesty. Fire it up. The color red, loads of lights, and wood (a symbol of fire) heat up your rep. It's also a good idea to place your TV here. Glass and mirrors (symbols for water) extinguish any power here.

Prosperity. More than money, this area refers to having the good things in life. Unsurprisingly, green and gold positively influence this area. But purple—the traditional color of royalty—is the major power broker here. Dust, dirt, and broken items conjure up the feeling of being—you guessed it—broke.

Family. In addition to steering your relationships with those bound by blood, this area also affects your daily necessities (rent money, mac 'n' cheese budget, chocolate, shoes). Use woods and greens here; anything metal or white pushes away the flow of easy conversation or relationships. It's a good idea to place family heirlooms in this area.

Skills and knowledge. How do you learn, store, and use information? You'll really want to amp up this area if you're in school, or if you are taking on a new project. If your kitchen falls into this zone, stock it with healthful foods that can feed the mind. Your bar cart should find another home, however, since it can cloud your judgment. Books do well here, clutter does not. Keep the area sleek and organized.

Health. This center area encompasses all aspects of your life in addition to your physical well-being. Earth elements, symbols of fruit, and muted tones enhance the elements of overall balance and health. The exception is wood, which translates into a disruption of the earth, and should be avoided here.

CULTURAL NOTIONS OF LUCK

No matter the culture, it's tradition to ward off bad luck from entering the home.

- Norse tradition equates acorns with good fortune. Put a single acorn on your windowsill to deflect lightning.
- The English and other Europeans hang an upward-facing horseshoe over the home's primary entrance to invite luck.
- Crosses ward off evil and are said to safeguard those who wear them. Hang one in any part of your home for protection.
- A nautical star is the symbol of guidance for sailors.
- In China, painting the front door red is considered good luck.
- A *mezuzah* (doorpost), traditionally a piece of parchment, is fastened to the right side of the doorframe of Jewish homes in keeping with *mitzvah* (moral law). Its placement symbolizes that God and the Torah (holy book) are entering.
- Elephants combat bad omens. Place one near your window to keep negative forces from entering.
- The cricket, a lucky symbol in many cultures, is the sign of prosperity, good fortune, and a bountiful harvest.
- The *hamsa*—an icon of a hand popular in North Africa and the Middle East—protects against the evil eye. Literally translated as "five," the *hamsa* is also known as the "hand of Fatima" or the "hand of Miriam."
- Across the colonial Americas, the pineapple was seen as a symbol of warm welcome and hospitality.

New home bonus: Three good luck tips for before you move in

1. Never carry an old broom into your new home. It carries remnants of the past.
2. Burn white sage. Waft the smoke around the entire home to banish any spirits or lurking negative energy.
3. Sprinkle salt at the doorsills and windows to prevent evil spirits from entering.

> *"Luck is believing you're lucky."*
> —TENNESSEE WILLIAMS

add interest

A truism of designing small spaces is that neutrals do wonders. The cool tones visually open the area to give an illusion of more room. But a bunch of flat-toned beige, cream, and oatmeal does not a welcoming home make. Texture does. You can easily make an ecru sofa and sand rug look inviting by introducing texture. Simply put, the concept is to include a wide variety of materials, fabrics, and tonal patterns. Introduce faux throws or area rugs, chenille blankets over the couch, or silk scarves as table runners, for example. Keep in mind that heavy textures can overwhelm a room, so limit the velvet to smaller accents.

See through

There's something oh-so *Casino*-era glam about furnishings made of Lucite. Acrylic glass resin, known commercially as Perspex, Plexiglas, and the aforementioned Lucite, is a lightweight, shatter-resistant alternative to glass. And furnishings made of this strong material take up no visual space. Their form and function is a boon for amplifying small quarters. Nesting tables are an awesome alternative to side tables and nightstands, and consoles appear to be floating above the floor when made of a sturdy Lucite. Such furnishings also appear sleek and glam, with a hint of artsy.

Avoid making your home look too theme park futuristic and stick to a handful of see-through pieces.

DOS AND DON'TS: CARING FOR LUCITE

While sturdy and flexible, some extra loving should be taken when cleaning your resin pieces.

Do use a soft, non-abrasive polishing cloth. A lint-free bamboo one can be less harsh than wipes made of other materials.

Do clean with hot soapy water. Your daily dish soap will do, or opt for the multi-purpose Castile soap. I love the lavender scent by Dr. Bonner. For more on scents see "Decoding Scents" on page 171.

Do dry with another non-abrasive cloth. A used one may have some unforeseen abrasives.

Don't use a paper towel. It can scratch the surface.

Don't use Windex or Fantastic. They can cloud the finish and deteriorate the acrylic over time.

Don't place acrylic pieces near direct heat sources. While nothing is likely to melt, it's better to be safe than sorry. Place rubber trivets on surfaces before placing hot plates on them.

accessorize

"The only thing that separates us from the animals is our ability to accessorize." Thank you, *Steel Magnolias*. It's the best way to display our personality, interests, likes, and passions. And that extends to the home. Sure, in a small space you'll want to decorate with accents that are functional and fashionable. Trays, baskets, and containers fit that bill. Utilize that oversize straw bag you scored at a market in Botswana to stash blankets by the sofa. Contain vases and candlesticks on a funky plastic tray. Store magazines in colorful baskets that meld with your décor vision. But in addition to using utility items, accessorize your home with pieces that reflect you. Display your prized possessions around your home, across different surfaces. Show off your collection of vintage globes along the credenza or use the space to show off the interesting vase you picked up on sale at your neighborhood boutique. However you choose to exhibit your accessories, it's a good idea to group them in threes. The look is less chaotic and more cohesive. Keep accent pieces dust-free to further reduce a cluttered look.

How to buy art

Buying art is an emotional (and sometimes pricey) proposition. Some tips to picking the right artwork for you:

Go with your gut. Pull the trigger if the piece speaks to you. Don't buy art because you think it will impress your neighbors. Choose something that creates an emotional response in you.

Look at design magazines (or websites). While pinning rooms, take extra notice of the art on the walls. Use it as a

---

ONLINE ART SOURCES

Tiny Showcase. Each week, the online gallery sells a new limited edition original work for as low as $20. Since 2005, the outfit has donated a portion of all sales to charities of the artists' choice.

Etsy. The enormous arts-and-crafts collective showcases a dizzying roster of artists across a variety of mediums.

Gilt Home. The high-end, members-only, flash-sale site showcases a variety of works by well-known names like Bansky and Parvez Taj next to a selection from up-and-comers likely to show at the next Art Basel.

OverstockArt.com. With less original works and more oil reproductions of the masters, this site has a shop-by-room feature and a cool function that allows you to upload a picture of your room to see how the piece fits.

Art River. A tightly edited selection of prints (some limited editions) from big-name modern masters.

MOMA Store. Prints by Warhol, Pollack, Dali, and other marquee modern artists sit next to designer furnishings, accessories, and arty takes on kitchen tools, among other housewares.

guide when shopping. When browsing, notice what you like. Is it watercolors or block prints? This is a good indication of what kind of artwork on which to focus your own collection.

Black-and-white compositions are easy to introduce, no matter your design sense. Vibrant graphic prints are also a good bet for art-buying beginners.

At local galleries, prints and photos tend to be lesser priced. Ask to take a piece on approval. You may have to pay something, but it can be refunded if the artwork in question doesn't work in your home.

Go to museums. Gift shops stock objects and prints from popular exhibits. Stay away from the Nighthawks and Mona Lisa repros in favor of some lesser known works.

Shop at student fairs. Large graphic abstract selections stand the test of time.

You can always reframe. Sleek, modern borders spruce up flea market finds and make concert posters appear more refined. Make multiple pieces look like part of a whole with coordinating frames.

Whatever you buy, the art should be in keeping with your home décor in both palette and size.

Three steps to create a gallery wall

A scattering of small wall accents creates the sense of clutter. Instead, place like-concept wall hangings to create a larger single appearance that can be the focal point of your room.

1. **Pick a theme.** To make the gallery cohesive, it's important to select items along the same theme or color palette. Black-and-white photos, for example, have an arty look, while images with a variety of blues add dimension. Also, select similar style frames that are simple. Ikea's Ribba series has mattes and various finishes for different print sizes.
2. **Define the space.** In small homes, the gallery concept works best on a focus wall (over the couch or behind the bed, for example). Start with two to four framed prints placed at the same height. (Note: Leave eight inches between the base of the frame and the top of the furniture.) Vary the distance and orientation between them, adding images up or out.
3. **Evolve.** Change out pieces; add new ones. As with every aspect of your home (and life), allow your collection to grow to fit your needs and interests.

Note: Need a more hands-on tutorial? Go to gradybug designs.com for a template kit.

Have a signature color

With all this neutral vibe going on to expand the look of your teensy home, you don't want to veer into hospital scenery from *Girl, Interrupted* territory. Having a signature color gives an accent to your home while showing off your personality. It facilitates your ability to coordinate accessories, art, and other décor elements so that they blend and create a cohesive look. Just remember that there can be too much

PANTONE COLOR OF THE YEAR

Since the year 2000, the first name in color, Pantone (the company that specializes in pigment production and owns a patented matching system), has declared an annual hue that permeates the zeitgeist.

- 2013 Emerald
- 2012 Tangerine Tango
- 2011 Honeysuckle
- 2010 Turquoise
- 2009 Mimosa
- 2008 Blue Iris
- 2007 Chili Pepper
- 2006 Sand Dollar
- 2005 Blue Turquoise
- 2004 Tigerlily
- 2003 Aqua Sky
- 2002 True Red
- 2001 Fuchsia Rose
- 2000 Cerulean

of a good thing. Overdoing the fire engine red touches can quickly turn your space into Toon Town.

Extend your signature hue to other areas of your life, like entertaining and gift giving. It saves time when you can consistently defer to the Kelly green ribbon. And it's a detail that people will remember—every girl knows the quality of a gift inside a bright blue box and those red envelopes let everyone know the newest release is in it.

DECODING COLORS

White signifies innocence, purity, and goodness. Some cultures use white as the color of mourning.

Gold is the color of wealth and prosperity.

Black, actually the absence of color, is associated with power, authority, evil, and, in recent times, elegance.

Yellow, the color of the sun, is often associated with happiness. It also symbolizes peace. In literature, the tone has illustrated women with hysteria.

Blue imparts tranquility. However, some say it increases productivity, which is why the hue is also associated with corporate cultures. Those shades are most often the cold tones; others impart a sense of peace.

Brown is earthy. It is also said to stimulate appetite.

Red is the color of both passion and caution. Some cultures see it as a lucky color. In Asia, many brides wear shades of red.

Green, in addition to money, reflects nature and fertility. It is said to symbolize both renewal and jealousy.

Purple is the color of royalty. It was said to have been Cleopatra's favorite.

"The purest and most thoughtful minds are those which love color the most."
—JOHN RUSKIN

go natural

Fact: Living things perk up the place. Not only are they a symbol for life and nature, but studies show that looking at plants can help alleviate the symptoms of stress and encourage relaxation. Some researchers have found that people with plants in their environment are more productive. Plus, plants can boost the oxygen levels in your house. Group plants together or along the windowsills. Place them in unexpected places like in the bathroom or on a bookcase to add interest to your décor scheme. Treat yourself to fresh flowers on a regular basis—it will add color and a bit of cheer. Remove dead plants or flowers immediately; they're dust-collectors and create bad juju. Consider using fruit as an accent. Place clementines, lemons, or apples in a squat vase as a display on your table or desk. Taking the fruit off the countertop is a space-saver and all-over enhancer.

"I must have flowers, always and always."
—CLAUDE MONET

Kill-proof plants

You don't need a membership to the garden club to keep some healthy greenery in your home.

Note: Less is more. In general, over-watering is worse than under-watering.

Air plants. Don't let the name fool you, these mini plants still need to be watered. Dampen the roots and leaves once or twice a week. Flaccid, rolled, or wrinkled leaves are a sign of dehydration.

Aloe Vera and succulents. These juice-hoarders love bright light and need water about once a week. Never let the plants sit in water—they will rot from the root up.

Bamboo. Said to bring luck and good fortune, these Asian plants like indirect sunlight and at least an inch of water around the red roots and stones in a vase.

Cacti. Just because these are native to arid areas doesn't mean they don't drink H_2O. They do, but only when the plant is a bit shriveled. Leave out of direct sunlight.

THREE STEPS TO CARE FOR FRESH-CUT FLOWERS

1. Keep it simple. Choose a single type of flower in a single color. No matter the bloom, it'll still look chic.

2. Keep it small. Trim stems on an angle and place in a smaller vessel than you would originally think. A large vase needs loads of blooms. A vintage juice glass is a great alternative.

3. Keep it clear. Leaves under the waterline cause rot more quickly. Change the water every two days. (Use a turkey baster to suck up the liquid.) And add fresh flower food or an aspirin with new water.

Spider plants. The cats of plants because they seem to have multiple lives, these sturdy guys love sunlight (a yellowish tinge on leaves signifies the want for more). Water the roots every two to three days, or when the soil is dry to touch.

Kitchen herb garden

Herbs—you need them to make your food (and cocktails) more flavorful. A bunch of your favorites make a nice house-warming gift.

Gather some terracotta pots. The material allows the plants and soil proper aeration. Place mini ones on a single tray to keep your indoor garden looking sleek and purposeful.

Mix up the soil. A healthy combo of two parts soil, one part sand, and a touch of lime is optimal for the health of your plants. Avoid the mess of blending it yourself and ask your local gardening center for a mix.

Let the sunshine in. Herbs do best with loads of light. Many, however, don't like direct sunlight, so place by a window, not in it.

Hydrate. If the soil is dry, your plant needs water. Feed your herbs with plant food about once every two weeks.

Enjoy! Use scissors to snip the leaves whenever you need to add basil to your recipe.

room-by-room décor solutions

Bedroom

You want this room to be dreamy, but that doesn't mean you have to cut down on its utility.

JUST FLOAT

There's no need to sacrifice a bedside table and reading lamp just because your bedroom is a refashioned closet. Utilize your wall space. Cut a floating shelf to an appropriate size and affix it to the wall beside the bed. Or mount a skinny horizontal bookcase. Lamps can be secured to the headboard or wall. If you are really short on space, invest in a storage bed with shelving on the side of the headboard.

MOVE THE PEGBOARD WALL OUT OF THE KITCHEN

Mount the material on any wall for extra storage of books, bags, scarves, or those knick-knacks you just can't part with. It's also great as a headboard. (How to: Cut down a pegboard to between 2 x 4 or 4 x 4. Using drywall anchors, screw through the pegboard and secure to the wall. Paint the board. Add hardware and floating shelves as desired.)

THREE STEPS TO MAKE THE BED—PROPERLY

Tossing the covers onto the bed doesn't cut it. Creating a neat bed (think: "military-style" and "hospital corners") also creates peace of mind. Here's how:

1. Start with a blank slate. Lay a fitted sheet on top of the mattress. Make sure each corner properly encircles those of the mattress. Tuck the hems of the sheet tightly under the mattress.

2. Evenly spread a flat sheet over the folded one. The pattern should be facing inward (or the "wrong" way). Align the top of the sheet to the headboard and make sure the ends extend beyond the foot of the bed. Standing by the center of the bed at the foot, pull the sheet hem toward you into a crease. Fold down to form a triangle and pull taut before tucking under the mattress. Repeat on the other side. Smooth away any wrinkles.

3. Fold over the top sheet a couple of inches away from the headboard. Lay out a duvet and top with pillows.

DOWNSIZE

Consider swapping out a queen-size bed for a full. Select a non-headboard, platform style to eliminate the need for a box spring. You can retain adequate under-the-bed storage space, while occupying less space.

Kitchen

With just a couple of tricks you can make your kitchen work harder for you.

ADD AN ISLAND

More than a surface area for prepping, the kitchen island can help with storage needs while also serving as a breakfast bar. Choose one with ample shelving and a sturdy finish, such as a butcher block. Put it on wheels to move in or out of the kitchen as needed.

LET THERE BE LIGHT

A well-lit kitchen appears bigger. Affix lights under your cabinets. Add a glass (or a reflective) backsplash to further amplify the illusion of space. Or consider hanging a chandelier. The delicate light can enhance a cramped kitchen by drawing the eye upward. Traditional candelabra styles impart an air of sophistication; a sputnik has a mod, urban look. Master the amount of light with a dimmer.

MAKE DIAGONALS

Lay floor tiles on a diagonal to enhance the illusion of more space. It's a visual trick that moves the eye away from strict horizontals and small corners. Keep the pattern simple and use tiles made from natural materials.

Living/Dining room

You'll probably be spending a lot of time in this space, so you want it to feel good.

DOUBLE UP

Opt out of a single coffee table and use two side tables or ottomans instead. Unlike the single and often chunkier piece, the doubles can be easily moved out of the way for parties. Make sure they are the same height and design to keep the look sleek and pulled together.

AIM HIGH

When selecting a daybed or sleeper sofa, look for one with a high and sturdy back. It is more formal looking than the low-sling styles and will give your home less of a dorm-room vibe. Don't forget the seat test. Sit on the cushions to ensure they are firm. Single cushion styles tend to give way less than the separated pillow types. If ordering online, see if you can find a brick and mortar outpost to do the seat test. Returning furniture after it has been delivered can be a hassle.

DRAW A CIRCLE

Balance all the straight lines and sleek angles you've implemented with a few round pieces. Moroccan poufs, circular side tables, and round coffee tables allow the flow of your home to feel more organic. And invest in a round leafed dining table. Such furniture pieces also counteract any sensation of living in an alley that so many straight lines may evoke.

Bathroom

Creating a great bathroom can make any apartment feel better.

MOVE IN

Amp up the function of your washroom with some non-traditional bathroom furniture. If the space allows, add a chest of drawers to store towels, linens, and perhaps your unmentionables. Use the upper drawers for toiletries and other accessories. A bookcase also makes a fabulous linen storage space, as does a small curio cabinet. A sturdy chair can work as well. Side tables are also handy. Use one to display hand soaps, perfumes, and candles. Stash your toilet paper in the drawers.

SEE CLEARLY

Clunky shower doors and opaque glass can make a space feel smaller. Switch them out with clear glass. You'll expand the sensation of leeway by about three feet—an enormous amount in tight quarters. Choose a door without a heavy frame.

PICK UP

Maximize your floor space by moving your bathmat. When not in use, store it over the side of the tub. Or roll it up and stash under the sink. By having it off the floor, you'll enhance the appearance of space.

PART THREE:
ENTERTAINING

"In wine there is wisdom, in beer there is freedom, in water there is bacteria."
—BENJAMIN FRANKLIN

overnight guests

In the olden days, people stayed at taverns or set up camp under the stars. During America's Gilded Age, aristocrats entertained overnight guests in their grand homes. Now your friends are taking a page out of Edith Wharton and bunking in with you, albeit without the glamorous balls. You can, however, ensure your guests have just as amazing a time even though you're short a lady's maid and a butler. The key to having overnight guests is to make them feel welcome enough that you appear as the most gracious hostess ever, but not so much that they overstay that welcome. Like most things in life, the devil is in the details. Providing the right linens, activities, and meals ensure happy guests and a happier you.

> *"Guests, like fish, begin to smell after*
> *three days."*
> —BENJAMIN FRANKLIN

Communicate

Before your out-of-towners descend on your home, hammer out the details of their stay. How long will they be with you? Will they be seeing other friends while in town? Get

WHAT'S A GUEST?

The dictionary definition:

- One who is a recipient of hospitality at the home or table of another.
- One to whom entertainment or hospitality has been extended by another in the role of host or hostess, as a party.
- One who pays for meals or accommodations at a restaurant, hotel, or other establishment; a patron.
- A distinguished visitor to whom the hospitality of an institution, city, or government is extended.
- A visiting performer, speaker, or contestant as on a radio or television program.

Origins of "Guest"

- Old English giest for stranger, enemy; related to Old Norse gestr, which dates to before 900; Gothic gasts, Old Saxon, Old German gast, Old Slavonic gostî

(Some) Synonyms for Guest

- bedfellow, boarder, boon companion, caller, client, companion, company, confidant, confidante, crasher, customer, dinner guest, drop-in, ephemera, fellow, frequenter, habitué, hanger-on, houseguest, inmate, invitee, lodger, mate, messmate, out-of-towner, partaker, partaker of hospitality, patron, recipient, recipient of one's bounty, regular caller, renter, roomer, sharer, sojourner, tenant, transient, vacationer, visitant, visitor

to know their goals and expectations for the trip. If your guests are planning on seeing a Broadway show or trying to get into a Lakers game, tickets may need to be purchased ahead of time. If you don't have the space in your schedule to procure such items, email your guests the best ticket-getting sources. Also, let them know your schedule. If you have to work or take an important exam, advise your guests ahead of time and make suggestions as to activities during that time slot. "I've got to meet my study group for an hour the day before you leave, would you like to see the library where we meet? Its architecture is pretty cool," for example. Also, consider looping your friends into your usual day-to-day routine; consider extending an invitation to join you in your yoga class or book club meeting.

> *"What is there more kindly than the feeling between host and guest?"*
> —AESCHYLUS, ANCIENT GREEK PLAYWRIGHT

Create an itinerary

The key to having a minor guest footprint all over your place is to get them out of there as much as possible. For significantly less mess, encourage your guests to do stuff off-site. For every person that cross-references travel guidebooks to figure out the most interesting sites in your area, there's one that can't name the major metropolitan airport they're flying into. So, create a mini-tour. There's no need to be bossy about it, simply mention cool art installations, your favorite coffee shops, or any walking paths you think your guests may enjoy. It is also a good idea to include a few activities that are free (your local museum on Friday night and the movie night on the beach). Have maps on hand (the laminated ones by Streetwise are easy to clean, store, and reuse), as well as a local guidebook. In permanent marker, highlight your local subway stops, bus access points, or highway exits. Also write your cell phone number on it and a list of taxi providers. Tailor your itinerary suggestions for your guests—sports fans may want to know about the backstage tours at Fenway, fashion freaks will love hearing about the new consignment boutique near your office—and the gracious hostess in you hits it out of the park.

> *"Guests bring good luck with them."*
> —TURKISH PROVERB

Invite in twos

Wait up, hold a minute, did you just read that correctly? The quick answer is: Yes. Admittedly, it seems counterintuitive; double the guest amount and double the space they occupy. OK, that's true, but the value in having a couple of overnight visitors versus a single is in their ability to entertain each other. Together, they'll be able to go sightseeing, which takes the pressure off of you to entertain 24/7.

Three rules to overnight guest if you have roomies

1. **Ask.** Clear any invitees with your roommate. It is as much her space as yours. Discuss arrival and departure dates (they should be firm), as well as sleeping arrangements.

WORLD'S 10 MOST VISITED TOURIST SITES

The world's iconic spots are on every traveler's must-see list. If you live near one, be prepared for a field trip with your guests or give them insider tips on the best (read: crowd-free) times to visit.

1. *Times Square, New York City:* 39 million visitors a year
2. *National Mall and Memorial Parks, Washington D.C.:* more than 35 million visitors a year
3. *Trafalgar Square, London:* more than 25 million visitors a year
4. *Magic Kingdom, Lake Buena Vista, Florida:* 17 million visitors a year
5. *Disneyland Park, Anaheim, California:* 14.7 million visitors a year
6. *Niagara Falls:* 14 million visitors a year
7. *Fisherman's Wharf and Golden Gate Bridge, San Francisco:* 13 million visitors a year
8. *Tokyo Disneyland and DisneySea, Japan:* 13 million visitors a year
9. *Notre Dame Cathedral, Paris:* 10.6 million visitors a year
10. *Disneyland Paris, France:* 10.6 million visitors a year

2. **Respect.** If appropriate, alert your guests to your roommate's habits (she works nights, so keep it down during the day). In the bathroom and kitchen, steer your peeps away from her belongings. (See "Stock the fridge" on page 125 and "Create a bathroom caddy" on page 127.) Ditto for her gadgets.

3. **Include.** No one likes to feel like a third (or fifth!) wheel: Even if you aren't BFFs, invite your roomie. Have her tag along on your visit to the neighborhood park or to check out the installation you heard she's been interested in seeing. There's no need to extend an invitation for every single activity, just the ones you know she'll he'll enjoy.

Make a set of keys

Yes, your guests are here to visit with you, but they are also here to see what your awesome city has to offer. Provide them with keys to your castle and they won't feel as tied down to your needs and vice versa. Assign a storage spot for your guest keys, either with their linens or tech center.

Centralize the technology

In today's iWorld, hosting overnight guests also means dealing with wires—gobs of them. Set up a charging station next to an open outlet or electrical strip. Assign a tray or a shallow media box for all things guest tech. If your guest is messy, clearly label the tech center with a neon sticky. Keep your WiFi password there, as well as any remote and DVR instructions your guest may need.

No one wants to experience a what-happened-to-my-*Parenthood*-episodes!? meltdown.

TRAVEL APPS

Consider adding a list of some or all of these handy travel apps in your guest tech center. They're great to use on the road or when you are at home base.

Weather Channel. No matter how many times your local news station praises the power of the Doppler radar, it rarely seems to be on target. This free app for every kind of handheld device gives forecasts by the hour and for the next ten days.

OpenTable. Think of this as the assistant you never had. The free-across-devices app allows you to snag reservations at the best area restaurants and emails you the confirmation.

Yelp. Looking for hot haute foodie spots? Employ this app, a loyal restaurant review site where users are honest with both the praises and the pans.

Uber. A cashless personal driver? Sign me up! Register on Uber's company website and request a cab via the app at any time. Text messages confirm the car's estimated time of arrival and when it has pulled up. Your credit card on file means never having to pay the driver directly.

MetrO. Like its cousin HopStop (which is limited to major American cities), this freebie is all about helping you navigate the public transportation system like a local. Best routes and travel times are clearly mapped out when you key in your origin and destination.

Free WiFi Finder. You know Starbucks is always good for a hotspot. But if you're in a pinch, use this free for Android and Apple tool to do exactly what its name indicates—pinpoint the open (and gratis) WiFi networks in your immediate area.

Bonus: Google Translate. In a foreign country? This app listens and repeats phrases and words in more than sixty-five languages. Ask "what's for dinner," for example and the app will tell you, "*ce qui est pour le dîner?*"

Smile

A happy host is a gracious host. Welcome your guests with genuine gusto. If you've properly prepared your home (and expectations), the visit will be fun (as well as painless). Enjoy your company and enjoy showing them your city. Upon arrival, review your guests' plans for their stay. Be flexible with any additions or subtractions. Don't feel pressure to do absolutely everything on their must-do list. If you've seen Strawberry Fields once a week for the last three years, agree to meet them afterward for a decadent sundae at the famous ice cream parlor around the corner.

> *"Visits always give pleasure—if not the arrival,*
> *the departure."*
> —PORTUGUESE PROVERB

Clear out

Use the advent of guests as an excuse to clean up and check in with some of the organizing methods you perfected in Part One. Remove excess clutter from any rooms or areas that your guests will be using. Also consider moving some of your furniture around. Now, I'm not suggesting you change the position of your couch—although now that we're on the subject, do you think it would look better in front of the window? This is more about reexamining the flow of your home in consideration for more bodies. Think about how you and your guests are going to pass each other in the hall. If you

THE LOW-DOWN ON SHEETS

Bamboo. Celebrated for its green sensibility, this cloth is fashioned from fine fibers of the grass-like plant. Sheets made of bamboo are soft to the touch and don't wrinkle.

Egyptian cotton. True to its name, this material is exclusively sourced in the North African country. Its strength, sumptuousness, and longevity are all thanks to Egypt's growing season. To amp up the luxe feel, most Egyptian cotton sheets have a thread count of at least 200.

Silk fiber. The most swish of all sheets are made of the extra-strong, extra-long, extra-soft, naturally woven fibers of the silk worm. The tradition of fashioning sheets from the delicate-to-the-touch material dates back 3,000 years.

Cotton jersey. Unlike most sheet materials, jersey (and its cousin flannel) is measured by ounces of material per square

have a credenza jutting into the path from your bedroom to your bathroom, for example, maybe it needs a new position. Or perhaps your dining table needs to swing over in a different direction to make space for the air mattress and suitcases. In the bathroom, assign a particular portion of the sink top for your guests' Dopp kit, and don't forget to have extra TP in plain view. Designate a similar area in the kitchen and office area for a tech center (see page 36). Aim to do all the heavy lifting at least three days before the arrival of your guests to ensure the new layout works.

yard of fabric, which explains the cost-friendly aspect. Made of blended cottons, the feel becomes softer over time and is often used for children's bedding.

Muslin. The tough version of cotton is strong, yet a bit rough to the touch. Sheets made of muslin have a lower thread count than most at 128 to about 140. Also preferred for children's bedding, muslin sheets tend to pill after multiple washings.

Percale. Wrinkle-haters choose this mid-thread count material, which is composed of a cotton-polyester blend, and therefore stays crease-free. The cloth is tightly woven and holds up against multiple washings.

Linen. Hypoallergenic and antibacterial, this natural fiber is fashioned from cotton. Although it feels luxurious to the touch, linen tends to wrinkle and needs to be treated gently.

Create a guest room

If you're lucky enough to have a room with a door that can be closed, assign it as guest quarters, even if it's just for this moment. Move your desk to the corner of the room and allow enough floor space for an air mattress to be blown up. Prep the space and linens prior to your guests' arrival so you can enjoy the visit (see "Three Steps to Make the Bed—Properly" on page 103). If you can, clear out a drawer or two in the room for your guests to utilize. Or assign a tucked-away corner as a suitcase storage spot. Use the seat of an extra chair as a side table and place a few city magazines and books about the local area on top. Also consider putting a task lamp, a bud vase (a repurposed juice glass filled with three rose buds), and a bottle of water on the chair seat.

Now, if you are in the sans-extra-room corner, you can still delineate a guest-specific space. If your couch or daybed is serving as the guest room, repurpose the side table as a bedside one. Lay out the mags, books, and water there. And carve out a bit of floor space for the guest baggage. Protect your floor with a pretty fabric remnant or beach towel—it'll also clearly demark the space. If you are using the couch as a guest bed, place the folded sheets on the back, to indicate the storage spot throughout the length of the stay. Show your guests the mechanics of the air mattress, sofa bed, or trundle. Bo Concept makes cool ottoman-bed convertibles. A roll-away feather bed is another great guest bed alternative. It can be folded and stored when not in use.

Always have more blankets at the ready—offer the decorative throws from your couch. Consider pulling the living room curtains closed for a better sleep.

Invest in a rolling rack

It can be used to hang wet laundry, as a coat rack for your next party, and a closet for your out-of-town guests. What's more, you can position the rack as a privacy shield for your pals who are camping out on an air mattress or couch. Big box retailers like Kmart sell collapsible racks that can be stored under your bed or sofa when not in use.

Switch places

If you are entertaining a couple or a late sleeper, you may consider donating your bedroom for the stay. Now don't be a martyr about it, it can actually help keep your home tidy. By giving your guests a room with a door, you'll be keeping their stuff out of the living room and out of sight. You'll also give them a sense of privacy. Place any clothes you may need on your rolling rack, in a tidy pile in the bathroom, or in your entryway (see page 54). Sleeping on the sofa may feel a bit like a vacation at home—you can watch TV from bed. And you'll have the freedom to wake early for your AM FlyWheel without having to tiptoe over an extended sleeper sofa. Older guests (read: your parents or in-laws) will certainly sleep more soundly in a real bed. *Note:* If you have a roommate, this is the best solution for hosting overnighters.

Make precious private

Even if your guest isn't a bull type in a china shop, he may not tread as carefully as you. Move your grandmother's Tiffany lamp and other delicate pieces out of reach. Place them on higher shelves of secure stationary storage. Bookcases and credenzas may get bumped. Similarly, remove

TOWELS BY THE NUMBERS

Bath towel. Most commonly made of terry, the absorbent (and most common size) rectangular-size cloth measures about 30 inches by 58 inches and is used post-shower, swim, or bath.

Bath sheet. A bit bigger at 35 inches by 60 inches, the bath sheet has the same use.

Hand towel. Made of the same material, this rectangular drying cloth measures about 16 inches by 24 inches. True to its name, it's used for the hands, although because of its size many people use it to dry the face as well.

Beach towel. Usually measuring longer than a bath towel, but not as wide as a bath sheet, the beach towel is generally used as a place to lie or sit upon when stretched over the ground or sand.

Sports towel. This ultra-absorbent synthetic cloth is used by competitive swimmers. Once saturated it can still absorb water after being wrung out. Microfiber towels have a similar ability to absorb, while drying in a flash, which makes the lightweight, synthetic material popular at campsites and among backpackers.

any items you deem intimate from your public spaces. Stash them in your bureau or inside the closet.

Wash up

Dust bunnies are not invited. It should go without saying, (but I'm reminding just in case), before you open your

Tea towel. Also known as a dishtowel, this rectangular cloth was traditionally made of linen. In many 18th century English homes, the servants were barred from drying fragile china, instead the woman of the house used this delicate towel.

Turkish towel. It is widely believed that the modern towel was invented in Turkey. This term refers to a longer towel made of a rough material that is fashioned in uncut loops, which are so tightly wound that they don't show indentations.

Oshibori. Literally a "hot towel," this small finger towel is presented to diners before the meal at Japanese restaurants. Some airlines distribute the folded, heated cloths to passengers on international flights.

Towel animals. Although their origin is unknown, many attribute Carnival Cruise lines as the first company to fashion animal shapes from folded towels at turndown service. Akin to origami, the practice is now quite common among the cruise lines and many all-inclusive hotel chains. The most popular configuration is a dove, the most complicated a monkey.

home, the floors should be swept, the bookcases dusted, and the clutter contained. But you should also pay attention to your linens. No one likes to sleep in storage-scented sheets. Do a quick load of your sheets and towels before your guests' arrival. Toss an all-natural sachet in your signature scent in the dryer. (Trader Joe's sells earth-friendly reusable ones in a variety of scents.) In lieu of folding, roll sheets and towels—it not only takes up less space, it also prevents wrinkling. Consider assigning a certain towel set color to each guest. It eliminates confusion and ensures nobody will be using yours.

Make rules

You don't need to be a bossy boots about it. Make like a job interview: Turn your shoebox—albeit cute—living status into a strength. Upon welcoming your guests, provide some snacks (see "Insta-party foods" on page 163) and do the grand tour. Along the way, highlight anything you want your guests to do or observe in your happiest tone ever. For example: "Here's the bathroom. As you can see it's Barbie-size, so after your shower, please place the bathmat over the tub and your towel over the curtain bar." Make similar statements for storing linens and luggage. If you're afraid of noise, blame the neighbors. "Hey guys, the dude downstairs is a crazy-bird about foot steps. He does the broom bang no matter the hour, so if you can keep it down, that would make my life easier." Aim for no more than five rules—too many and your guests may forget. If you

CAN I HELP?

The Dos and Don'ts to responding to the age-old question.

Do: Be clear. Make specific requests that are easy for your guest to handle. Ask her to set out the silverware for dinner and clearly explain where the knives are kept. Have him bus the table and pile the dishes next to the sink.

Do: Bring it up. Don't be afraid to ask your guest to help you peel potatoes/feed the dog/fold up the sofa bed. She's crashing on your couch free of charge, and should be able to help out in a minimal way. You're not being a taskmaster by asking for help when you need it (or want to chat while you're getting the salad ready).

Don't: Lie. Demurring the request for help because you feel bad doesn't make you any more gracious. In fact, it can make you a bit resentful.

Don't: Go overboard. Unless your guest has taken up permanent residence on your air mattress, asking that she complete chores above the menial can be a burden on her. It can also be more of a hassle for you. Fielding the litany of "where is it" questions and the "how does it work" queries on a big task can be more time-consuming than doing it yourself.

require things like coasters and slippers, show them to your guests upon arrival to your home. Paper slippers are easy to store under the sink. Got any weird tics to your plumbing or shower? Explicitly break down any sort of details.

Assign a water glass

You know that more than one glass in the sink of a mini-house looks like a thousand discarded drinking vessels. Give your guests pint-size glasses that are theirs to use for agua throughout the length of their stay. Show them your water dispenser and any nuances to using it. Hint: Check Target's sale section for colorful options that are easy to distinguish from each other. While you're at it, encourage your

PARTY HISTORY FUN FACTS

Tribal warriors entertained in their homes. Greeks did, too.

The ancient pashtun people who inhabited today's Afghanistan and Pakistan held proper hospitality in the highest regard. In fact, it was a tenant of the tribal "code of life" that dates to the first millennium BC. Tribes, which at one time stretched from modern-day India to Turkey, were required to grant asylum to anyone who asked. The demonstration of hospitality was done and expected without the notion of recompense.

The ancient Greeks regarded *xenia* (hospitality) as a divine right. The concept of *xenia* is inclusive of both guests and hosts. It states that a host must provide food, drink, and a bath, as well as a parting gift. The guest, in turn, is expected to be courteous and not a burden.

The ancient Irish had a similar view of hospitality. Celtic law required a host provide food, drink, a bath, and entertainment to anyone who appeared on his doorstep. A

pals to help themselves to the snacks and breakfast food. See "Stock the fridge" below for more info.

Stock the fridge

Let's be clear, you aren't your houseguest's mom, so there's no need to have endless pans of baked ziti and a lifetime supply of tuna salad sandwiches on Wonder with the crusts cut off. But having some key items in the pantry is a gracious and time-saving gesture. If you've already got the snacks for an insta-party (see page 163), simply supplement with

guest, for his part, was expected to abstain from violence or arguments after accepting the hospitality. The law aimed to encourage trade throughout Eire.

There's a five-step approach to the traditional Hindu duty of hospitality called *atithi devo bhavah* (loosely translated as "the guest is god"). The rituals include the host's offering of fragrance, to put the guest in a good mood; a lamp, to signify the availability of the host; fruit and milk, for nourishment; rice, which is often dyed and smudged at the forehead as a symbol of unity; and flowers, a gesture of goodwill that symbolizes the making of sweet memories.

The term "southern hospitality" was first used mid-1830s. It referred to the openness and willingness for Americans living south of the Mason-Dixon line to provide enough food for anyone who may be around at mealtime. Properly addressing one another (as sir or ma'am) and being chivalrous are also part of the gentile ways.

a few personalized options. For example, if your pal is wild about coffee, have some beans from a local roaster all set. Or if your cousin is super excited about cheese, introduce her to the latest offering from your CSA. She'll appreciate the personalized gesture. Also, even if you don't eat it yourself, get light breakfast food. It's the cheapest and easiest to stock and the most difficult one to forage when you're out of your element. Select easy-on-the-prep-time choices like muffins, bagels, whole pieces of fruit, and cold cereal. Do a kitchen tour, pointing out the way to use certain (necessary) appliances—coffee pot, toaster, dishwasher—as well as the food and snacks that are open season.

> *"We dare not trust our wit for making our house pleasant to our friend, so we buy ice cream."*
> —RALPH WALDO EMERSON

Set a menu

Pare down your prep hours and increase your visiting time by deciding on meal options ahead of time. Shop and prep anything ahead of your guests' arrival. Heating up a quiche is a lot easier than whipping it up while attending to your guests' needs. When you coordinate the visit with your out-of-towner, assess how many meals you'll be eating at home and what, if any, food allergies need to be considered. Then you can accurately make your shopping list.

Create a bathroom caddy

What is it about toiletry bags that make them seem inherently chaotic? You should have already demarcated a place for your friend's things in the bathroom, but going a step further benefits you both. Set out a bath basket filled with guest-only goodies. Consider getting a waterproof container that can be taken in and out of the shower—upright plastic silverware trays work as well as a caddy. Or choose a mesh bag kit (Amazon and Bed, Bath & Beyond carry such kits targeted toward college kids). Place a few things your guests may need in the bag—travel sizes of shampoo and moisturizer, extra hair elastics, a mini bar of soap, individual packs of Advil. Always have an extra toothbrush and travel-size paste on hand. It's something your guest is sure to forget. Encourage your out-of-towners to leave their stuff in the caddy as well; it'll control the mess. After her departure, toss any half-used bottles. Revaluate your caddy whenever you do a clutter clean out (see page 7 in Part One). When not in use, stash the caddy under the sink or in a closet. Don't have an inch of space for yet another item to store? Utilize a shower curtain with built-in pockets.

Tidy up

Now this doesn't mean you follow your guests around with a bottle of Fantastik and a roll of paper towels. It's more about controlling the mess. If your couch surfers are staying for more than a night, help them store the air mattress or trundle the first thing in the morning. And employ their assistance. If necessary, explain the mechanics of the sofa bed, again. Replace toiletries in their basket. And mention it as you do so. But do it in a non-nag way. "Hey, I put the toothpaste in the guest caddy, so you can find it. My bathroom is small, but it's easy to lose track of things," for example. Remember, you are a gracious host, not a harpie, so do it all with a smile.

Ditch the cooking

Another way to offer a customized experience is in the food you choose to serve. Instead of mussing up the kitchen every evening of the stay, whip out the take-out menus. Each person can choose what she likes, and since you're only using plates, not pots and more pots, clean-up is a cinch. Gracious hostess bonus: You can introduce your guests to cuisine they've never tried. Avoid the lure to serve the meal straight from the take-out containers. Instead, bring out your pretty plates and real silver.

Note: Unless you're hosting a Food Network star or a major type A, decline your guest's offer to cook; the clean-up will likely end up with you. Try suggesting a favorite brunch place or dinner spot instead.

> *"It is not the quantity of the meat,*
> *but the cheerfulness of the guests,*
> *which makes the feast."*
> —EDWARD HYDE

TAKEOUT BY THE NUMBERS

- The average American eats 76% of meals at home. That number includes take-out, says the National Restaurant Association.
- Adults consumed, on average, 11.3% of their daily calories from fast food during the years 2007–2010. Fifteen percent of those people were ages 20–39.
- There are approximately three billion pizzas sold in the United States each year. Americans eat 350 slices per second, according to the National Association of Pizza Operators.
- Thirteen percent of American consumers have used the Internet to place an order for take-out or delivery according to the National Restaurant Association.
- The five most popular days for pizza delivery are Super Bowl Sunday, New Year's Day, New Year's Eve, Halloween, and Thanksgiving Eve.
- Italian, Mexican, Chinese, and pizza were the most popular restaurant types in 2011, according to a survey conducted by Living Social and Mandela Research.

Follow up

A good guest will follow up with a thank you note or email. But you can beat them to the punch with a quick note to make sure she arrived home safely. Text about how much you enjoyed the visit, specifically call out a memorable moment or two, and possibly attach a photo. Now is also the time to plant the reciprocation seed. If you had a difficult visit, suggest the next time you meet up, it take place on a more neutral playing field.

Put it back

OK, that was fun, but now—woo-hoo!—your home is your own sweet home again. Immediately upon your guest's departure, put away your only-for-couch-surfers items. Store the visitors' tech center (page 113) and activity ideas info (page 110) for your next houseguest, as well as the bath caddy. Strip the bed, wash the linens, and take out the trash. If you have time, do more than a speed clean and place any furniture you moved back to its original position (unless of course, the pieces work better in the new spot).

big party, small everything else

Whether game day, holidays, or a just cause day, entertaining at home is an extension of your personality. But doing so in a cramped apartment can seem a bit daunting—I mean, hello, where are all these people going to fit? A few tweaks to your home's layout and a quick repurpose of your items and, voilà, your home is hosting-ready. Also, have a few standby entertaining tricks in your arsenal.

Make an assessment

Take a good, long look at your studio/dorm room/800-square-foot two bedroom and calculate exactly how many people can fit comfortably for your event. According to domestic doyenne Martha Stewart, the average room can comfortable fit thirty people (or one person per five to six square feet), standing. Keep that number in mind when drafting a guest list (see "Create a Guest List" on page 132). Also, think about the theme or goal of your party. Is it a casual Sunday Patriots viewing session? Or is it a house-warming cocktail? Game nights, baby showers, and Oscars parties will need more seating than a New Year's bash or a no-gifts birthday celebration, so edit your guest list accordingly. In general, you can expect a 20% decline rate on your invites. Imagine your guests moving around the space and dancing to the latest Beyoncé hit. Or see them socializing by the buffet or chili bowl. What does your party look like? In this pre-planning stage think about any furniture changes and décor additions. Get broad strokes about menu, music, and, if applicable, activities. It's also the time to get your party-throwing team together if you're going to need help.

> *"Hear no evil, speak no evil—and you'll never be invited to a party."*
> —OSCAR WILDE

Create a guest list

There are just a few basic steps you should consider when making a guest list.

Mix it up. A room full of law students may lead to a nuanced discussion of civil procedure; a bunch of bloggers could concentrate on analytics. Make sure your list has a healthy assortment of professions, hobbies, and passions. Ensure that although they have different interests, they'll enjoy socializing together. For example, your roommate from your abroad program in Ecuador may enjoy learning about your pal from Pilates' stint as a Spanish teacher.

Host a "party" person. Everyone knows that one guy who is a hit in every social situation. His energy is infective and he's good at getting people talking, taking the all-hands-on-deck pressure off of you.

Only have desirables. Your party isn't the time to mend fences with a co-worker. Keep your guest list filled with people who want to be at your party and who you get along with well. The only exception is your neighbors (see "Invite the neighbors" on page 144).

Set the scene

As with interior design, flow is a tenant of a great party. Yes, it's the impression of open space in your home, but in this case, it's literally how your guests move throughout your home and interact with each other. So unless you are a professional party house, chances are the way you've got your small space arranged isn't the most conducive for a festive gathering of more than one. Translation: You may have to move some things around. Now there's no need to uproot your sofa and bed (unless of course you have a Murphy that can so easily be stored into the wall). But if you're in a studio, consider covering your bed with a festive sheet or tablecloth to transform it from your sleeping cocoon into a more party-appropriate seating area. This will also protect your duvet from becoming fiesta-worn. Or toss loads of throw pillows on the mattress to invoke the idea of a laid-back lounge. Move anything that's in the middle of the room—coffee tables, ottomans, etc.—out toward the walls. And utilize the surface space for décor items, extended buffet stations, or lean-tos for guests. Seating should also be close to the wall to encourage mingling and movement. But, note, this can be a tricky one. Too many occupied seats along the wall runs the risk of looking seventh grade dance instead of super-fun party of the year. (A good rule is to have less chairs than people.) Consider unfolding chairs as the need arises. You also want to ensure you've got ample space around the bar and food areas. One way to do this is by separating the buffet and cocktail stations.

Clean it up

It may seem a bit duh, but it's very important to keep your home tidy for guests. Hosting a party in a messy space is

---

WHAT'S A PARTY?

Party: A gathering of people who have been invited by a host for the purpose of socializing, conversation, or recreation. Food and beverages are typically served.

Celebration: A party held in honor of a certain person, day, or occasion.

Shower: Thrown in honor of a specific guest upon marrying or having a baby, it is a gathering to specifically gift the person of honor. Historically, the practice came from the dowry tradition, when a poor woman's family may not have the money to enter marriage. It also mirrors the trousseau (hope chest) custom of colonial America.

Tea party: A late-afternoon gathering characterized by the use of formal serving- and silverware and a women-only guest list.

Soirée: From the same French word meaning "evening period" and Latin *sero* meaning "late," this is a reception or party held at night.

akin to a scene from *Animal House*. Skip the speed clean in favor for the down-and-dirty, full-on scrubbing session. Aim to complete the project a day or two before the event. That way you won't be mopping the kitchen floor minutes before your guests arrive. It'll also give you time to prepare food, hang décor, and do other last-minute preps. Do a quickie speed clean (see "Speed Clean in Three Steps" on page 7) just before you don your pretty party dress or special occasion duds.

Cocktail party: First used in 1928, the term is exactly what it is: an informal or formal gathering in which cocktails are served.

Dinner party: An occasion where dinner is served, either at a buffet or formal table seating.

Potluck: Traditionally speaking, the term refers to food provided for an unexpected guest or "what's in the fridge surprise." It then morphed into a meal with no particular menu, for which Irish women cooked together in a single pot. It now refers to an event to which attendees are asked to bring a dish or meal.

Mixer: A get-together with the specific purpose for guests to meet one another in an informal setting.

Kaffeklatsch: An informal gathering over coffee, which generally includes a gossip session.

Clambake: Yes, it's an outdoor party on the beach where seafood is cooked over heated rocks, but it's also refers to a noisy social gathering.

Go double duty

Sounds familiar, doesn't it? Well, it *is* a mantra for dwellers of spatially challenged homes. If you're entertaining in a teensy crib, you've got to exploit all your resources and repurpose. Clear out a shelf in your bookcase for plates, napkins, and dishes. Use the top of a credenza as a buffet. Dress up your daybed to be more conducive for seating. And consider filling your squeaky-clean tub with ice and bevies. Another trick: Throw a tablecloth over an ironing board (if you have one) and use as a serving table, or utilize the surface of your desk.

keep it clear

As we discussed in the first section, clutter makes everything appear smaller. Keep surfaces free and clear. In the bathroom, restrict the items on your counter to hand soap, a candle, and flowers. Store everything else under the sink. Take the same approach to your kitchen and desk. If you're repurposing any surfaces, limit the items on them to the party's function. Extend the clear concept to hallways and center gathering area of your party (see "Set the scene" on page 133 for more information). You want people to be able to move and socialize with ease.

Embrace the bar concept

Even if you realistically have the space for a sit-down meal for eight (OK, a tight eight), consider giving everything the buffet treatment. It takes the pressure off of a single spot, helps your company move around, and gives your party—you guessed it—flow. The bar concept differs a bit from the straight-on buffet as it's an interactive selection of food or drink options. Think: Make your own sundae party. It invites guests to create their favorite dishes and customize selections to their taste. Giving the option to personalize their food and drinks also scores points in the gracious host column, as it shows that you are interested in their likes and wants. It also eases up on your prep time in the kitchen.

More than three bar concepts, however, and you've got a bottleneck at the food area.

DIY bars

CHAMPAGNE BAR

There are few things that say "fun times," like a little bit of sparkle.

- Set two opened bottles of champagne at the end of your cocktail serving area. At least one should be chilled in either a wine chiller or a bucket of ice. (Don't have a bucket? Use your sink or fill a colander with ice and set over a bowl.) Set an unopened bottle there too—it invites guests to help themselves. (Read: Not interrupt you when you are attending to other people.) Store the other bottles readily accessible in the fridge.
- Set out some glasses. Plastic flutes are an easy option. Make sure you've properly attached the bottoms.
- Offer two or three juice mixers. Cranberry juice, pear juice, and lemonade are all yummy options.
- In ramekins or juice glasses, set out a few fresh fruit options. Strawberries are the expected accruement, but I prefer pomegranate seeds, blueberries, and peach slices.
- To curb costs, get a case of Prosecco (Astoria retails for about $10 a bottle versus the $65 of Veuve Clicquot). Often, a wine store will negotiate the price when you purchase a case.

THREE STEPS TO THE BEST PLAYLIST

1. Set goals. What's your party's jam? Are you hosting a *Mad Men*–style cocktail party or is it your annual Yankee swap? Select a genre of tunes that jibe with your gathering's vibe.
2. Make sets. Think of the rhythm and pacing of songs. Group them together in sets of three. Be sure to include crowd favorites and some classic party tunes.
3. Label. Every crowd has a wannabe DJ. Keep your playlists clearly marked so DJ Mess It Up doesn't accidentally put on your homage to Mandy Patinkin.

Note: The music's volume should be loud enough so that people have to talk over it slightly.

BRUSCHETTA BAR

- Slice a toasted baguette or make garlic crostini (see recipe on page 152). Present on a wooden cutting board or other flat surface.
- Place three topping choices in small prep cups or ramekins. Set a coffee-size spoon or cheese knife in each.

dos and don'ts for being a gracious host or hostess

Do: Create ice breakers
Don't: Make them hokey

There's a difference between introducing two guests who you think will hit it off because they share a love for the Spanish national soccer team and going around the room so everyone at your party can name their favorite *Girls* character and why. Facilitate socializing by presenting guests with conversation points that link them to each other.

Do: Make guests feel appreciated

Mingle with your guests and aim to spend a significant amount of time visiting with everyone. Thank them for coming. And personally escort each guest to the door when she is ready to leave. If appropriate, have a plate of leftovers prepped for the taking. Also, have a taxi number at your fingertips for guests who may not be able to drive.

Do: Enjoy yourself

As the hostess or host, you're the party's focal point. Translation: You set the tone. Yes, you're responsible for the food and drink, but if you're locked in the kitchen or trapped behind the bar, you're working, not partying. Looking and feeling stressed out about everyone's fun actually makes everyone else feel the same way. Instead, enjoy a cocktail, dance with your friends, and have a good time.

Don't: Overlook the details

The difference between a great bash and a *meh* one is in the fine print. Make sure you've properly stocked the bar and have enough food. And assess your guests' needs. Don't let someone sit in the corner tweeting alone—unless it's to Insta the fun she's having.

Don't: Be rigid

Don't be Lucy from *Peanuts*. Just because you were stoked on playing a killer round of Celebrity, doesn't mean everyone's down with it. Be willing to massage your plans on the fly. If you were expecting a game night, but everyone would rather watch the presidential debate instead, go for it. Guests will appreciate your flexibility.

> *"If you wou'd have guests merry with your cheer /*
> *Be so yourself / Or so at least appear."*
> —BENJAMIN FRANKLIN

keeping it cool

There are some basic things you can do to make the party a lot easier on you before, during, and after the raucous good time.

Create a coat closet

If you've got a separate bedroom, you can assign your bed as the jacket catchall. In a studio that's probably not an option. Clear out a specific area (your landing strip chair, page 14, is a good option) to store coats and bags. Your entryway (see page 54) is another great one. If you have a rolling rack, situate it with extra hangers in a conspicuous spot. Or consider clearing off your desk and placing folded coats there. Don't hang the coats on your shower curtain rod—it won't be able to handle the weight.

Also, spread out a welcome mat. Many apartment buildings have rules against storing anything outside your door. But having a welcome mat at your door for one night won't get you fined. Guests are likely to wipe off their feet before entering if there's a mat at the entrance. Ikea has a variety of styles that don't look too temporary.

Stay out of the kitchen

As we've discussed, a big part of your role as host(ess) with the most(ess) is interacting with your guests and having a good time yourself. Make sure everything is totally prepared before guests arrive. Have your bar and buffet stocked. If you plan on bringing out more food at a later point in the evening, have it prepped and plated. Light all the candles and set your dimmers on the lamps. Give yourself enough time to pour a cocktail or glass of lemon water before guests arrive. Running around until the doorbell rings is just stressful.

Control the chaos

There's pretty much nothing worse to dealing with a party post mortem than having to clean up a complete and total disaster zone. Plan ahead and you'll avoid such headaches. Place your garbage can in a conspicuous place. Label it as well as your recycling bins. Point them out to your guests to help you in your efforts. Every now and again do a quick sweep of the buffet and bar. Combine anything as needed, and trash used paper plates and napkins. Immediately place dirty dishes in the dishwasher to avoid piling up in the sink. An overflowing sink is a number one space cruncher.

Invite the neighbors

Unless you're hosting a shower for a specific guest of honor, the neighborly thing to do is include the people who live in the building. Extend a genuine invitation to your immediate neighbors (directly above, directly below, and on either side). Depending on your relationship they'll decide on whether their presence is appropriate. But it is their choice to make. Slip a note or formal invitation under their doors with all the pertinent info. Include your phone number as well. You'd rather they call you with a noise complaint instead of the police.

DO I KNOW YOU?

How to deal with people you didn't invite:

If your friend shows up with an uninvited plus one, don't make a big deal out of it. A gracious host always makes more room at the table. Don't show your annoyance and comment on the lack of food. Take the high road: Make that girl who stole your roomie's boyfriend feel as comfortable as those you invited. There's an exception, however. If the person is a drug dealer, privately explain to your guest that you are uncomfortable. And firmly ask that he escort his uninvited plus one elsewhere.

"Nothing makes you more tolerant of a neighbor's noisy party than being there."
—FRANKLIN P. JONES

How to save a dying party

There are few things worse than an energy-free fiesta. Here are a few pointers on how to pump up the jam:

Circulate the food and the word. Mingle with guests and encourage them to speak with each other as you pass around your favorite dishes.

Dim the lights. Give a more intimate feel to your fiesta. Consider breaking out a special bottle of champagne to make the party feel more special. Make sure you acknowledge the guest who provided the bubbly and introduce her to some others. Use it as a conversation starter.

In the words of Lady Gaga, "just dance." Pump up the boogie-down tunes and get two or three people to join you in a dance-off. It'll get the energy level up.

decorate

Dress up your place to reflect the festive nature of your gathering. Now, this doesn't mean stringing four-leaf clovers from the rafters, plastering shamrock decals on the walls and putting green food coloring in your beer. Instead, use accent pieces to evoke your party's theme. Colorful cocktail napkins do the trick, as do festive table runners or repurposed scarves. Choose flowers that reflect the season—red roses are perfect for your Christmas party and Fourth of July gathering, deep orange Gerber daisies are great for a Thanksgiving or harvest dinner. Also play with centerpiece ideas. Place pinecones, lemons, or Christmas ornaments in clear, geometric vases, for example. And don't forget the candles. Keep tapers and pillars the same color throughout your apartment (white and metallics are best). Hint: Stash tapers in the freezer to prevent wax dripping.

prep the bathroom

The powder room set-up is just as important as the décor and buffet. It's an extension of your sense of hospitality to have a perfectly presented bathroom. If you haven't already, clear off your countertop. Stash your toothbrush in the vanity and place your perfume bottles under the sink. Set out a festive hand towel or individual guest napkins, and get your everyday bath towel out of there. You don't want guests using it. If you haven't any space, toss it in your hamper. Avoid the gooey soap situation and put a pump soap in your signature scent on the sink. Place a few buds in a juice glass and light a candle on the back of the toilet or on an out-of-the way shelf. Last, but definitely not least, have enough toilet paper. There's nothing more embarrassing for a guest than having to hunt down TP. Take it out of the packaging and place in an oversize glass cylinder vase or gather in a galvanized bucket in clear view of the toilet.

feeding the masses (aka party platters)

In a sentence: go small (plates). Tapas, mezze, picada, it's all the same concept—appetizer-size servings of a variety of dishes, or in restaurant-speak, small plates. It's a culinary notion (much like the make-your-own bruschetta below) that gives diners a mix of various tastes. As a hostess, it helps you in the clean-up department—most tapas are finger foods, which means no utensils. The key to pulling off a great mezze is having bite-size foods with tastes that complement and coordinate with each other. Doing so also self-edits your shopping list.

Pretty (easy) party recipes

These super simple recipes created by Alison Mahoney, The Singing Baker, will give you more time to prep your small space and yourself for your bash of the year.

Tomato Bruschetta   *Makes 8–10 servings*

2 pints of multi-colored grape tomatoes

¼ cup olive oil

fresh basil

salt and pepper

Cut the tomatoes into quarters and chop basil. Place in a bowl and sprinkle salt and pepper. Drizzle ¼ cup of the oil and mix thoroughly. Let sit and marinate in its juices for at least 30 minutes before serving.

White Bean Bruschetta   *Makes 8–10 servings*

1 (16-ounce) can of cannellini beans

1 small red onion, finely chopped

1 clove of garlic, grated

¼ teaspoon red pepper

salt and pepper to taste

⅓ cup olive oil

2–3 sprigs fresh rosemary, roughly chopped

Drain the can of cannellini beans and place into a medium-size bowl. Add onion. Grate or finely slice the garlic into a paste and add to the bowl. Sprinkle with red pepper, salt, and pepper. Pour in the oil and rosemary and mix together with a spoon. Marinate for at least 30 minutes prior to serving.

Pea Puree   *Makes 10–12 servings*

1 (10-ounce) bag of frozen peas

⅓ cup Parmesan cheese

1 tablespoon fresh lemon juice

salt and pepper to taste

⅓ cup olive oil

Thaw the frozen peas in hot water. Strain peas and place into a small food processor along with the Parmesan cheese, lemon juice, salt, and pepper. Give the peas a quick spin in the food processor and then slowly stream in the olive oil until entirely incorporated and smooth. Store up to 3 days in the refrigerator.

TAPAS AROUND THE WORLD

Although the origin is still up for debate, **tapas** were served up with any order of beer and wine at most bars across Spain for centuries. Today the term refers to a variety of hot (meatballs, fried calamari, sautéed mushrooms) and cold (tortialla española, jamón serrano, Manchego cheese) dishes that are emblematic of Spain's gastronomy and are served off a menu for dinner or a late/light lunch.

- Literally translated as "snack," **picada** is generally a selection of cold dishes—olives, ham, cheese—in Argentina.
- Served from Greece to Syria, the **mezze** is a celebration of the bounty of Mediterranean cuisine. Although the selections vary from county to county, nearly every mezze showcases local cheese and seafood, cured meats, olives, and marinated vegetables.
- Linked to both the tradition of tea tasting and the trade of the famous Silk Road, **dim sum** refers to individual or bite-size portions of food. Many dim sum restaurants have rotating carts filled with steamer baskets offering an array of dumplings, buns, pot stickers, and other finger foods, such as spare ribs and spring rolls.
- In Chile, restaurants offer **tablas**, hot and cold samples of food most often served on an oversize wooden dish.

Tablas are generally thematic (Italian, sweet, vegetarian).

- On the Hawaiian islands, meeting up for cocktails includes enjoying a **pupu platter**, or a group of appetizers. The big plates meant for sharing often feature egg rolls, spare ribs, fried wontons, and beef teriyaki.
- **Thali**, which means "plate" in Hindi, is an array of various dishes served in small bowls placed on a round tray served in India and Nepal. Rice, dahl (lentils), yogurt sauce, and chutney accompany bowls of vegetarian or meat-based selections.
- Finger sandwiches, olives, and other snack-like dishes called **cicchitti** are traditionally served as a late lunch, with local wine at bars in Venice.
- Although translated as "side dish," Korea's **banchan** are small plates of shared food that are served along with individual servings of rice. The number of banchan presented in the center of a Korean table directly corresponds to the number of people seated.
- Technically, the Italian **antipasto** is the first course of a meal. But it's side-by-side presentation of cured meats, various cheeses, anchovies, olives, mushrooms, pickled veggies, and more on a single serving dish is why some people group antipasti plates with tapas.

Crostini *Makes 24 pieces*

1 baguette
3 cloves of garlic
olive oil

Preheat oven to 350°F. Slice the baguette in ¼-inch diagonal slices. Rub each slice of bread with garlic and place on a baking sheet. Lightly drizzle bread slices with oil. Toast in the oven for 10–15 minutes, until the bread is crispy. Serve with Tomato Bruschetta (page 148), White Bean Bruschetta (page 149), and Pea Puree (page 149).

MAKE LABELS

OMG the vegan is about to bite into a prosciutto-stuffed fig and you are on the other side of the room dancing. There's nothing you can do to save her in this moment, but having your food and cocktail options properly labeled takes the guess-work out of the gluten-, dairy-, peanut-free allergy decoding. There's no need to invest in escort cards (although West Elm always has cute ones and Anthropologie often has a robust selection in their sale section). Opt for heavy stock paper—I always use index cards—folded and cut down to size. With a Sharpie, clearly label the dish or cocktail: for example, Spinach salad with roasted Brussels sprouts, shaved parmesan, and olive oil; Margarita with fresh squeezed lime juice. To up the festive feeling, add a sticker or decal to the corner of your label. If you have a roommate, you may also consider labeling doors that are not guest-accessible.

Mini Quiche   *Makes 24*

3 eggs, slightly beaten

1½ cups heavy cream

2 tablespoons flour

2 cups cheddar cheese, shredded

1 pinch of nutmeg

2 tablespoons instant minced onion

1 (10-ounce) package of frozen spinach, thawed

Preheat oven to 350°F. Spray a mini cupcake tin with non-stick cooking spray. In a medium-size bowl, beat the eggs and cream together until well blended. Add the flour, cheese, nutmeg, and minced onion. Squeeze all of the water out of the thawed spinach and place a table-spoon of spinach at the bottom of each cupcake cup. Pour egg mixture over spinach and place in the oven for 15–18 minutes or until set. Let stand for 15 minutes before serving.

Mix and match your standard offering with quickie varia-tions:

- Replace two cups of Swiss cheese for the cheddar cheese.

- Add ¼ of a pound of ham (cold cut) cut into small bite-size squares.

- Replace crumbled feta cheese and bite-size pieces of asparagus instead of cheddar and spinach.

Put it on a stick

Finger foods give you the easiest clean-up. And without having to hunt down utensils, your guests are more likely to enjoy your food. Varying the presentation can make your selections appear more appetizing. Sure you can use skewers for meats, but you can also place colorful veggies and fruits on a stick for a bit of flair.

Greek Salad Skewers *Makes 16*

¼ cup feta cheese, cut into ¼-inch cubes

8 grape tomatoes, cut in half

8 pitted Kalamata olives, cut in half

¼ cup olive oil

¼ teaspoon of salt and pepper

¼ teaspoon dried oregano

1 cucumber

16 small skewers

In a medium-size bowl, toss the feta, tomatoes, olives, olive oil, salt, pepper, and oregano. Set aside. On the diagonal, slice the cucumber ¼ inch thick. Cut each slice in half and add to the bowl. Let mixture stand for at least 15 minutes before placing on the skewers, alternating tomato, cheese, cucumber, olive.

Caprese Salad Skewers *Makes 16*

½ cup Balsamic vinegar

16 mini buffalo mozzarella balls (bocconcini)

16 grape or cherry tomatoes cut in half

16 fresh basil leaves

olive oil

16 small skewers

Pour vinegar into a sauce pan over medium-high heat and bring to a boil. Remove from heat when the vinegar is thick, syrupy, and shiny. Set aside. Alternate cheese, tomato, and basil leaf on skewers. Drizzle with olive oil and the balsamic syrup.

Watermelon Skewers *Makes 16*

2 cups watermelon, cut into ½-inch cubes

½ cup feta cheese, cut into ½-inch cubes

2 teaspoons lime juice

a pinch of salt

¼ cup fresh mint leaves

16 small skewers

In a bowl, toss watermelon, feta, lime juice, and salt and mix together. Chill for 15 minutes. Alternate watermelon, mint leaf, and feta on skewers.

"I'm into very colorful food.
Obviously lots of flavor, but I think we eat with our
eyes first, so it has to look great.
The presentation has to be great."
—GIADA DE LAURENTIIS

have signature desserts

Having a few marquee desserts and dishes makes planning a party a snap. As with colors and scents, signature dishes are your calling card (or your brand, dear blogger). It's also an enticement to guests. If you're known for the best peanut butter chocolate chip cookies across three counties, it's your milkshake—it brings all the boys to the yard. Aim to have a few sweet and a few savory treats in your arsenal. Stick with your mix-and-match concept to offer a variety of tastes.

"Cooking is like love. It should be entered into
with abandon or not at all."
—HARRIET VON HORNE

Mini Chocolate Cupcake *Makes 24*

1 cup milk (can substitute soy, almond, or rice milk)

1 teaspoon apple cider vinegar

¾ cup sugar

1½ teaspoons vanilla extract

⅓ cup grapeseed oil (or any light-flavored oil)

1 cup flour

⅓ cup plus 2 heaping tablespoons cocoa

¾ teaspoon baking soda

½ teaspoon baking powder

¼ teaspoon salt

Preheat oven to 350°F. Pour the milk and apple cider vinegar into a measuring cup and set aside for 3 minutes. Then pour the milk mixture into a medium-size bowl. Mix in sugar and vanilla with your mixer set on low, slowly adding oil. Sift the flour, cocoa, baking soda, baking powder, and salt, over the liquid ingredients. Mix on medium speed until the ingredients come together. Place decorative mini-cupcake liners in a mini-cupcake tin. Fill

SERVING PIECES EVERY HOME SHOULD OWN

Trays. Platters can hold cold cuts, cooked meats, veggies, pasta, and fruit. Repurpose (and wash!) trays that you use for décor.

Large bowls. Salad, chips, and pretty much anything can be presented in mixing bowls.

Cereal bowls. A good substitution for ramekins, cereal bowls can hold condiments, nuts, and olives.

Six silver oversize spoons. Keep the pattern basic. Mix-and-match plates blend well together, not so for silver. Add two or three serving forks, depending on your needs.

A set of cheese knives. Use the soft cheese spreaders for dips, as well as Brie. The hardier knives can slice your "home-made" pizza (see recipe on page 161) some wine-dipped salami, and, of course, cheese.

each halfway with batter. Bake for 10–12 minutes or until a toothpick comes out clean. Let cool before frosting.

Basic Chocolate Buttercream Frosting

½ cup butter (2 sticks, one warmed, one cool)

1 teaspoon vanilla extract

4 cups confectioner's sugar, sifted and divided

3–5 teaspoons of water

⅓ cup cocoa

Mix together heated butter and vanilla. Fold in cold butter, 2 cups of sifted confectioner's sugar and 2 teaspoons of water. Mix on low. Add remaining sifted sugar, cocoa, and 2 tablespoons of water, and mix on high for 5 minutes or until you have a creamy texture. Add another teaspoon of water if the frosting is too stiff.

Shortbread Cookies 3 Ways   *Makes 24 cookies*

COOKIES

½ cup butter (2 sticks), room temperature

½ cup granulated or confectioner's sugar

2 cups flour

½ teaspoon salt

¼ cup dried cranberries

¼ cup chopped walnuts

zest of one orange

TOPPINGS

⅓ cup white chocolate, melted

⅓ cup bittersweet chocolate, melted

1 tablespoon orange juice

1–2 teaspoons grape-seed oil

⅓ cup dark chocolate, melted

Preheat oven to 350°F. Break up butter in a bowl. Add sugar, and beat together until light and fluffy. Add flour and salt and mix until the batter comes together. Separate the dough into thirds.

In the first section, add cranberries and walnuts. Roll into a log. Chill and slice into ¼-inch pieces. Place on a parchment-paper-lined baking sheet.

Add the orange zest to the second section of batter. Roll into a log. Chill and slice into ¼-inch pieces. Place on a parchment-paper-lined baking sheet.

Use your favorite cookie cutter to create shapes with the final section of dough. (Choose ones that coordinate with your party's theme.) Place on a parchment-paper-lined baking sheet.

Bake each section of dough for 7–10 minutes or until the edges are very light brown. Cool cookies before decorating.

Drizzle melted white chocolate onto the cranberry-walnut cookies.

Mix melted bittersweet chocolate, orange juice, and grape-seed oil. Dip orange-flavored cookies into the mixture.

Dip shaped cookies into melted dark chocolate.

Apple Crisp *Makes 8 servings*

6 Granny Smith apples

3 tablespoons butter, divided

1 teaspoon cinnamon

pinch of nutmeg

½ teaspoon ginger

pinch of salt

¼ cup water

¼ cup brown sugar

1 cup rolled oats

¼ cup flour

Preheat oven to 350°F. Slice apples into ¼-inch slices. Melt ½ tablespoon of butter in a skillet on medium heat. Add apples, cinnamon, nutmeg, ginger, and salt. Sauté until fruit is a little soft. Add water and cover. Cook for another 3 minutes. Remove from heat and pour mixture into a casserole dish. In a small bowl, fold together remaining butter, brown sugar, oats, and flour with a fork until the mixture is moist, but still crumbly. Pour dry ingredient mixture on top of apples. Cover with tin foil and bake for 15 minutes. Uncover and bake for another 15 minutes. Serve warm with bourbon whipped cream.

Bourbon Whipped Cream

1 cup heavy cream

2 tablespoons confectioner's sugar

1–2 capfuls of bourbon (or to taste)

In a chilled bowl, blend the heavy cream and confectioner's sugar on high until soft peaks form. Add bourbon and mix until high stiff peaks form. Note: Don't over-mix, unless you want super sweet butter.

do some
semi-homemade

Another way to pare down your prep time is to use what your mother gave you—pre-made ingredients. If you live in a mini-home with a barely there kitchen that doesn't even have an oven, you'll have to go semi-homemade, so embrace it. As with your signature dishes, select a few key options that don't overwhelm with the "I came out of a box" vibe. Also, decant and use serving ware. No one will notice the paper plates you set out on the buffet if you present the noodle salad in a jadeite serving bowl. See "Dress it up" on page 164 for more info.

> *"People who love to eat are always*
> *the best people."*
> —JULIA CHILD

"Homemade" Pizza   *Makes 9 square pieces*

1 eggplant
olive oil
salt and pepper to taste
1 large red onion, sliced
1 package store-bought pizza dough

1 whole head of garlic, roasted

½ cup feta cheese

½ cup mozzarella, shredded

Preheat oven to 350°F. Slice eggplant into ¼-inch slices and brush with olive oil and sprinkle with salt and pepper. Place slices onto a baking sheet and roast in oven for 20 minutes or until caramelized. In a frying pan, sauté the red onion on medium-low heat until transparent and soft. Rub olive oil onto a sheet pan and stretch your room temperature pizza dough to fit the pan. Rub all of the roasted garlic into the dough and drizzle with oil. Fan roasted eggplant and caramelized onions over the dough and generously sprinkle with cheese. Bake in the oven for 30 minutes or until the dough is a golden brown. Let stand for 5–7 minutes before slicing and serving.

Mix and match your standard offering with quickie variations:

- Replace artichoke hearts for the eggplant and use ricotta cheese in place of the feta.
- Garnish with thinly sliced prosciutto, arugula, shaved Parmesan, and a light drizzle of lemon juice in place of the eggplant, feta and mozzarella.

Roasted Garlic

1 bulb of garlic

olive oil

Set oven to high broil. Slice off the top of the bulb of the garlic and drizzle with olive oil. Wrap in aluminum foil and broil for 30 minutes or until the garlic is golden and soft.

INSTA-PARTY FOODS

A good hostess is always ready for drive-by guests. Keep a few snacks on hand for those people who were just in the neighborhood.

Hummus. This tangy spread couples well with crunchy veggies and crackers of all kinds. Put between bread for a sandwich. Or keep a can of garbanzo beans in your cabinets. Add a bit of olive oil and garlic and blend well. Voila, hummus.

Rice crackers. These gluten-free discs pair well with hummus and cheese. They are also pretty tasty on their own.

A hard cheese. Spanish Manchego cheese seems so much chicer than cheddar, but either pairs well with almonds, dried fruit, and rice crackers.

Baby carrots. Dip in hummus or salsa.

Dried fruit. These sweet treats add color to any plate. Toss in a glass of Prosecco for a quickie champagne cocktail. Add with almonds to make a trail mix.

Almonds. Classier than peanuts, these nuts pair well with any sweet or salty snacks.

Grapes or fresh berries. Fresh fruit adds a pop of color, a hint of sophistication, and some proper nutrition to a plate.

Prosecco. Champagne's cheaper cousin wows the socks off of impromptu guests. Place in the freezer for about 10 minutes to chill.

Dress it up

It's all in the presentation—from job interviews to store-bought cupcakes, the key to making the best impression is enhancing the look. When entertaining, bring out the serving ware. Even bagged snacks look chic in the proper vessel. Put chips in a crystal bowl; display a store-bought crudité on a Lucite plate; arrange White Castle burgers on a silver tray. The pieces don't need to be all matchy-matchy to look good. They simply need to be sturdy and reflective of your personality. On each tray, display more food than you initially need. That way you won't have to refill throughout the night.

set the bar

Now that you've got the menu set, it's cocktail o'clock. The bar should be separate from the food so that people can access each without hassle. It's also a good idea to position the bar in the corner of the room to avoid any bottlenecking. Like other things in your small space, you can opt out of the full size. Instead of a fully loaded cocktail cart, offer guests beer, wine, and a signature drink prepped in a pitcher. The cocktail should jibe with the vibe of your fiesta. I love any version of the Bellini (the traditional, which was created at the glam Cipriani Hotel in Venice, is a mix of Prosecco and peach puree). And who doesn't find white wine sangria refreshing? If your best girlfriend is the grande dame type who simply can't imbibe anything except extra dirty martinis, gently remind her a day before the gathering that your menu doesn't include her cocktail of choice and she should plan accordingly. Don't forget to have non-alcoholic options. Sparkling juices are a great alternative.

You may also consider going clear with your beverage choices. In a small space, it's easy for a glass of red wine to get jostled and spill onto your neutral-toned couch. Keeping the cocktail choices simple can also help streamline your planning process.

*"Here's to the alcohol,
those rose colored glasses of life."*
—F. SCOTT FITZGERALD

Cocktail Recipes

Whiskey, like champagne, is a party powerhouse. Served neat it has a *Mad Men* throwback feel. It's easily blended into classy cocktails and it's fun to shoot with a Bud chaser (late night only, of course).

Whiskey Smash

This Mint Julep cousin is simpler to make and just as refreshing.

2–4 lemon wedges

4 mint leaves

1 ounce simple syrup (or 1 teaspoon fine sugar)

2 ounces bourbon whiskey

ice, to fill shaker

Muddle lemon and 3 mint leaves in a cocktail shaker. Add simple syrup and whiskey. Fill with ice, and shake vigorously for about 30 seconds. Strain and garnish with the remaining mint.

New York Sour

The amped-up Whiskey Sour has an air of sophistication that makes it appear more complicated.

2 ounces bourbon whiskey

1 ounce simple syrup (or 1 tsp fine sugar)

juice from 3–4 lemon wedges

ice, to fill shaker and glass

½ ounce fruity red wine (Shiraz or Malbec)

Pour the whiskey, simple syrup, and lemon juice in a cocktail shaker. Fill with ice, cover, and shake vigorously for about 30 seconds. Strain into a glass with fresh ice. Hold a spoon over the glass and pour the wine gently onto the spoon so the wine flows over and floats on top of the beverage.

Pickleback

This new-to-the-scene combo (it is believed to have launched in Brooklyn in 2006) is a refreshing—and different—taste that adds dimension to the liquor.

1 shot Irish whiskey

1 shot pickle juice (it's the brine from your everyday pickle jar!)

Pour whiskey and pickle juice into separate shot glasses. Drink the whiskey immediately followed by the pickle juice.

Punchbowl Cocktails

Mixing up a single takes time and can take your focus off your guests. Combine these cocktails pre-party and you'll have more time to boogie down.

French 75

The ultimate classic champagne cocktail, this concoction adds an air of sophistication to any gathering.

16 ounces gin

8 ounces freshly squeezed lemon juice

6 ounces simple syrup (or 6 teaspoons fine sugar)

½ teaspoon of grenadine (or bitters)

ice, to fill bowl

32 ounces dry champagne

In a punch bowl combine the gin, lemon juice, simple syrup, and grenadine. Stir well until blended. Just before serving, stir in ice and champagne.

White Wine Sangria

A twist on the traditional version means spills are worry-free.

2 ounces brandy

⅔ cup fine sugar

3 oranges, sliced

1 peach or nectarine, sliced

1 lime, sliced

1 lemon, sliced

ice, to fill bowl

2 bottles white wine

Combine brandy, sugar, and fruit. Stir and let stand overnight. Add ice and pour in wine just before serving. Mix well.

*Note: You can make this less boozy by subbing one bottle of wine with a ½ liter of club soda.

Rum Punch

Did two words ever go together so seamlessly? It's a party favorite for two reasons—it's a cinch to make, and it tastes like vacation.

1 cup fresh lime juice

3 cups light or amber rum

2 cups pineapple juice

2 cups orange juice

ice, to fill bowl or pitcher

fruit slices, for garnish

Pour all the ingredients into a bowl or pitcher. Chill for an hour in the refrigerator. Add ice and garnish with fruit of your choice, as much as you like.

have a signature scent

Lavender, vanilla, or sandalwood not only make your space feel more homey, they'll also camouflage any last minute cleaning you did before your parents/new boyfriend/old college roommate arrives. Now you don't need to get all séance-y with the candles; room sprays (organic ones, not the chemically smelling numbers) and reed diffusers also impart a delicate aroma. When you're hosting a party, strategically scatter candles around your home, adding to the ambiance. Also, avoid using the overhead lights. Use lamps in addition to the candles.

Why to invest in good-quality scents

It may seem silly to blow big bucks on candles, when you literally watch them burn. But there are a bunch of reasons to invest in your scents.

They're better for you. Lower-grade candles use cheaper wax, which can produce a lot of sooty smoke and burn with an oily smell. Look for candles made of soy. They're free of the toxins toluene and benzene.

The scents are just right. Cheap candles tend to have overly perfume-y scents and sour top notes. Tapers made of beeswax have a pleasant, faint aroma of honey.

They last longer. The cotton, braided wicks of expensive candles burn more evenly and slowly than their cheaper counterparts.

Their glasses are wider. Tapered jars trap air and don't let the scent circulate as evenly. Soot can also build up on the neck.

Note: Make your candle last—always clip the wick before lighting.

Candles are purchased by 70% of U.S. households, and are used at least once a week, according to the National Candle Association.

Decoding scents

Aromatherapy has a powerful effect on mood. Scents can help alleviate the effects of stress, anxiety, and depression.

Eucalyptus, Australia's most famous plant, is stimulating, cooling, and refreshing. It has been found to counteract the feelings of sluggishness and exhaustion.

Lavender's scent has a calming, sedative effect. Some studies have shown that the scent of lavender can promote sleepiness in those who suffer from insomnia. The aroma has been shown to increase brain waves associated with relaxation according to the Smell and Taste Foundation in Chicago.

Lemon oil has been linked to an improvement in alertness and concentration. It also alleviates the feelings of depression and anxiousness, according to research from Ohio State University.

Peppermint, in addition to soothing the respiratory system, is said to be energizing. It also promotes alertness and memory.

FAVORITE CANDLE BRANDS

Munio Candela: Made of pure soy wax with cotton and wood wicks, these earth-friendly candles are scented with wild herbs and packaged in recycled jars.

Diptyque Paris: The granddaddy of luxurious home fragrance, this French company offers an array of classic aromas, intoxicating blends, and limited-edition candles. Travel sizes and reed diffusers are a wallet-friendly way to enjoy the chic Parisian scents.

Archipelago: Hand-poured and long-lasting, the candles from this organic company are less expensive than the others on this list due to the varying percentages of pure soy used—it's never less than 70%.

Red Flower: The perfect apartment-size candles feature intoxicating aromas culled from fresh flowers, zesty fruits, and natural oils.

Mrs. Meyers: The green clean brand of-the-moment has a yummy selection of soy candles in the same scents—lavender, geranium, lemon verbena, basil—as its cruelty-free, organic household products.

Votivo: A pioneer in the luxury candle market, this company boasts some of the most recognizable scents—Red Currant, Amber, Sea Island Grapefruit—in candles, incense, room sprays, reed diffusers, and more.

Rosemary's scent can cause an increase in cognitive function in both speed and accuracy, according to a variety of studies. There's also evidence that rosemary is a mood-booster.

Ylang-ylang, a symbol of love and ever-lasting happiness in Madagascar, is said to uplift mood and outlook.

occasion-by-occasion solutions

Now that you know the basics on how to generally throw the best party ever, here are some details to make sure each kind of party you have will be a smashing success.

Brunch

Brunch is the perfect occasion to utilize the bar concept (see page 165). Cut bagels into fourths and toast some in the oven before guests arrive. Arrange them on a plate with hummus, cream cheese, Tofutti spread, lox, and peanut butter in ramekins close by. Make sure you set out a spoon or spread knife for each. Whip up a few frittatas or quiches (see recipe page 153) and serve them at room temperature, along with other goodies. The champagne bar (see page 138) works well, too. But really don't forget the coffee. People come to brunch expecting it and loads of it. Make a major pot of coffee and keep it hot in a thermal carafe. If you don't drink java, pick up a traveler pack at Dunkin Donuts. Again, create a coffee bar with milk options—skim, cream, and chocolate almond milk—and spices (cinnamon, sugar).

Birthday/Housewarming

Although traditionally these two events include gifts, it's considered rude to ask people for presents for yourself. Instead, treat either event simply as a "just 'cuz" party with your favorite tunes, foods, and décor. Keep in mind, however, that guests at a housewarming party, which is generally held within 120 days of moving in, expect a grand tour of the new place. Note: If your friends are the gift-giving types, specify "no gifts, please." Do you really need more clutter? If you're hosting a housewarming and need stuff, consider creating a registry.

Just because party

Host friends for a party just because and use all the tips you learned in the previous pages. To make it a little more memorable, infuse your fiesta to reflect the season or theme. Give away mini-candies at Halloween, make some gingerbread cookies at Christmas, and decorate with colorful Day of the Dead–flags on Cinco de Mayo.

Shower

Before coordinating the date and menu with the guest of honor (bride- or mama-to-be) define your space constraints. Clearly explain the buffet and bar layout, as well as where the present opening will happen. Section off an area away from your home's entrance for the gift collecting. Make sure there is enough space to place a chair. Your guest of honor should open gifts from that position. Ensure all guests have a clear view and, if necessary, scatter floor pillows so that everyone has a seat. Also discuss décor options with the bride; decorations should reflect the wedding theme, at least indirectly. Have flowers or fruit bowls in the color of her bridesmaid dresses or decorate the buffet area with nautical accents, for example. Keep the entire party well lit. (Note: If she prefers a sit-down experience, consider moving the celebration to a restaurant or event space.)

TRADITIONAL HOUSEWARMING GIFTS

The origins of "housewarming" are up for debate. Some point to medieval France and the celebration of the completion of a new home. Others talk of a Norse tradition akin to the 12 days of Christmas. Whatever the genesis, the act of opening one's home in celebration of its newness became wildly popular in the 1970s in America. If you're trying to figure out what to bring, or decipher a somewhat odd gift, you can refer to this list for some traditional gifts given to bless a house:

- Bread. That your cupboards will always be full.
- Broom. That your home will always be clean and free of evil spirits.
- Candles. That you may have light through the darkest times.

Bachelor party

Although a bit more in the debauchery realm, such fetes have similarities with the shower. You've got to scope out your space and bar constraints ahead of time. Loads of booze and little light are generally hallmarks of stag parties. Talk to your guest of honor about his preferred dates and activities of choice. If poker is high on the list, consider moving your furniture around to highlight a game table. If outside—ahem—entertainers are expected, prep the space ahead of time with a chair of honor at an easy-to-reach spot from the door.

- Coins. That you may receive luck and good fortune.
- Honey. That you may always enjoy the sweetness of life.
- Knives. That your home may always be protected from Intruders.
- Olive Oil. That you may be blessed with health and well-being.
- Plants. That your home may always have life.
- Rice. That your love may multiply.
- Salt. That life here may always have flavor.
- Wine. That you always have joy and never go thirsty.
- Wood. That your home will have stability, harmony, and peace.

Potluck

A six-pack and a potato may make the ideal Irish meal, but a pretty, balanced meal and a nice party it does not. Make a detailed list of what you want/need. Speak to your guests and play up their strengths. If your cousin doesn't know how to spell o-v-e-n, never mind how to turn one on, ask her to hit Whole Foods for their great vegan cake. Specify how many people you need to feed and what exactly you'd prefer, chocolate over coconut, for example. Set up the party using bar and buffet concepts and make sure you have enough plates, silverware, and serving ware. Also stock up on plastic containers to pack leftovers for everyone.

Holiday meal (Thanksgiving/Christmas)

This occasion is a bit more formal than the others and you may want to host people for a sit-down meal around a table. To increase your surface area, lay a piece of plywood over your desk or dining table. Cover with a festive tablecloth. In the kitchen, set up food buffet-style (it will keep the table clear). Store the plywood under your bed when not in use. Note: The ideal number of dinner party guests is six to eight. It keeps the conversation interesting, while not dividing it too much.

Game day/Awards night

Since the goal of the gathering is to watch TV, keep the food selections to a minimum. Make sure the tastes coordinate with each other and place them out of view of the television.

That way, those chatting at the buffet won't disrupt the game watching. Don't be ashamed to make your gathering BYOC (bring your own folding chair) if you don't have enough proper seating.

Impromptu

Ding, dong. No that isn't the opening sound of *House Hunters International*, it's your own doorbell. And a few friends just happened to stop by. If they give you the blessing of a text telling you they are around the corner, do a speed clean (see "Speed Clean in Three Steps" on page 7) and light candles in your signature scent (page 170). Spread a tablecloth over your credenza, desk, or dining table and decant your insta-snacks (see "Insta-Party Foods" on page 163) into serving dishes.

APPENDIX

apartment glossary

Learn the lingo to setting up your ideal *House Beautiful* with these key terms for space, decor, and the overall life in the fab lane you always dreamed of.

What's an apartment?

Broker-speak may seem like something of a foreign language. Read on for exactly what "a bachelor apartment" means.

Alcove studio: Just as the name infers, there's a niche that is often used as the bedroom area. "L studio" is another name for such a layout. Junior one-bedrooms are actually larger alcove studio apartments with an oversize, windowless recess accessed by a door. No matter the size, alcoves do not have closets.

Apartment building: A multi-story structure that houses three or more dwellings within a single building. Also called "apartment house," "block of flats," "tower block" and "high-rise" or, in Britain, "mansion block."

Convertible apartment: A studio, one-, or two-bedroom dwelling that allows for a temporary, pressurized wall to create more bedrooms. Also called "flex" or "flexible."

Duplex: An apartment of any size, split into two floors with an interior staircase. A Triplex is spread across three levels.

Efficiency: Another name for a studio, although this apartment tends to have cook tops in lieu of full stoves and is often smaller than a studio. In some markets, the efficiency is also called a "bachelor apartment."

Garden apartment: It's not a basement-level dwelling, but a multiple-unit low-rise residence having considerable lawn or garden space. In some cities, garden apartments are ground-floor abodes with outdoor space.

Junior four: A one-bedroom apartment, generally with one and a half bathrooms and a dining area that can be converted into a second bedroom.

Loft: Usually a large, open space, a loft apartment is part of a converted factory or warehouse. A loft tends to be a single room with oversize windows, high ceilings and limited built-in closets. Live/work lofts are exactly what it sounds like, spaces that are legally zoned for both conducting business and dwellings. So called "Soft Lofts," are units in newly constructed buildings that have open floor plans and high ceilings. They are also often referred to as "loft-style." "Hard Lofts" are apartments in converted factories.

One-bedroom: This denotation directly reflects what it is: an apartment with a separated bedroom and living area, divided by a door. Each has windows. And the bedroom has a closet or storage cubby.

One-bedroom, plus: A one-bedroom apartment with an additional, windowless (and often closet-less) alcove area.

Penthouse: Though technically this is a unit built into the edifice's rooftop and recessed a bit to have large terraces, it is often simply marketed as occupying the top floor.

Pied-à-terre: Literally translated from French as "foot on the ground," it refers to a part-time residence, generally an apartment in a large city that is used for part of or the entire work-week.

Railroad: Also referred to as a "shotgun apartment," the living space is divided into a series of adjacent rooms.

Studio: The smallest kind of living arrangement, the space encompasses the kitchen, living area and bedroom in a single area. The bathroom is separate.

Design 101

Save this cheat sheet to decoding scale and size:

Balance: The distribution of weight throughout the room. A space can be symmetrical (think: two wing chairs flanking a coffee table), which tends to be more formal looking, or asymmetrical, which can be achieved with the use of multiple small items placed across from a larger piece, such as a sofa.

Line: This refers to the physical space of the room. It can be augmented, diminished, or enhanced by using furnishings and accent pieces. Horizontal lines impart the sensation of relaxation; vertical ones are more formal; diagonals give the feeling of motion; and curves bring a softness to the room.

Proportion: The relationship between furnishings in the same space.

Rhythm: A little more esoteric and innate in terms of "getting" it, this element refers to the use of texture, pattern, and lines.

Scale: The proportion of furnishings in relation to your space. In some ways, it also speaks to the user's function. For example, a kid's chair would be out of scale in a childless home.

What's a couch?

Yeah, it's that comfy thing you sit on, but the distinctions don't end there.

Chesterfield: First commissioned by the 4th Earl of Chesterfield, this style sofa features the same height arms and back and quilted fabric, usually leather. In Canada, the term is often used interchangeably with "couch" and "sofa."

Couch: Originally from the middle French word *coucher* (to set in place or to lie down) this is the term commonly used in the U.S., Australia, and New Zealand. Traditionally, it refers to an armless, chaise-like piece of furniture with a tapered back.

Daybed: A cross between a bed and a couch, a daybed usually has a back, sides and a trundle (a mattress on a frame with casters that stores underneath).

Divan: During the Ottoman Empire, mattresses were laid along the floor or slightly raised on a platform or frame. In Europe in the mid-18th century, divans became backless, armless couches designed as a bed and often found in the boudoir. Today's divans most resemble the "fainting couches" of the 19th century, which have only one section of the back raised.

Futon: Generally cotton-filled, this mattress is used in a frame as a bed/sofa combo. The word originates from Japan and refers to traditional bedding that is stored during the day.

Settee: A medium-sized sofa with arms and a back, this term is often synonymous with a loveseat.

Sofa: Derived from a variety of sources—the Arabic *suffa* (carpet, divan), Turkish *sofa,* and the Italian *sofà* (raised carpet floor)—this term is defined as a long upholstered seat usually with arms and a back, and often convertible into a bed.

Squab: Sometimes used as a synonym for couch, this generally refers to a cushion for a sofa or chair.

What's a rug?

Although the origins differ (see page 83), the words "carpet" and "rug" are essentially interchangeable. In fact, the definition of the two words is exactly the same: a heavy fabric used as a floor covering. Techniques and fabrics, however, vary. Some of the popular options:

Braided: Synthetic or natural strands are placed together so that they appear to be woven. Braided rugs are most often found in area or accent sizes.

Embroidered: True to its name, this is a series of fiber stitches into another fabric base.

Hooked: The simplest style of rug is constructed by weaving strings of cloth through a mesh of sturdy fabric.

Needle felt: Generally used in commercial, high traffic areas, these carpets are made of fibers compressed onto a textile such as foam. They are often manufactured in China.

Tufted: The most common of carpet styles, these machine-made rugs are double bonded to the backing to have more stability and longer durability.

Woven: Produced on a loom, the pile (density of the carpet fibers) are evenly looped into the rug's backing. There are two styles of woven—plush or cut, which is bundles of yarn standing straight, and berber, which refers to a thicker yarn at even levels. They are generally made of natural fibers such as wool, jute, and sisal. Due to the labor-intensive nature, this technique often creates the most expensive type of rug.

Greeting a foreign exchange guest?

Como se dice "welcome" around the world:

Ahlan wa sahlan: Arabic
Huãnyíng: Chinese
Bienvenido: Spanish
Welkom: Dutch
Tervetuloa: Finnish
Bienvenue: French
Willkommen: German
Kalós orísate: Greek
Aloha: Hawaiian
Baruch haba: Hebrew
Benvenuto: Italian
Kangei: Japanese
Mile widziany: Polish
Dobro pozhalovat: Russian
Karibu: Swahili
Yin-dee-ton-rab: Thai

index

acknowledgments

Although a small space, nothing is created in a vacuum, and I'm grateful to those who have helped me on this project. Major props to my ground team—Maria Mahoney (for proofreading and research assistance), Iván Guillot Boyer (for late-night dinner making and some research assistance), Alison Mahoney, the Singing Baker, (for creating those yummy party recipes), and Bill Mahoney (just because). *Mil gracias* to my editor Katherine, who in addition to being super cool, made the process a breeze and had an amazing spidey sense of when I needed an encouraging email. This book wouldn't have been made if it weren't for the support and encouragement of Robin Westen. And a special thank you, Myrna Blyth, my Machu Picchu *companera*, for introducing us. Thanks also goes to the team at *Bridal Guide* for being so supportive and flexible.

about the author

Jenna Mahoney is a Brooklyn-based magazine editor and writer. She specializes in travel, weddings, beauty, and healthy lifestyles. She has been on staff at *Bridal Guide* and *Fitness*. Her work has appeared in *Shape*, *Self*, *Allure*, *Redbook*, and *New York Magazine*, among other magazines. Online, she has contributed to AOL's *That's Fit*, Sephora's *Beauty and the Blog*, *Betty Confidential*, and the *Tory Burch* blog.